FLOGGING THE QUILL

Crafting a Novel that Sells

Ray Rhamey

FtQ Press

www.FtQPress.com

ISBN 978-0-578-00935-3

Library of Congress Control Number: 2008910678

Copyediting by Dallen Rose
Design by Ray Rhamey

Contents

"A masterpiece of *showing* how to fix prose, not merely *telling*."

Chris, writer

As if rejection weren't enough.

This book is dedicated to writers who are climbing the steep and never-ending learning curve for writing novels, striving to learn and improve.

And to the "litblogosphere," the writer/editor/agent bloggers who inform us and teach us, and to those who once did but have faded away (we miss you, Mad Max Perkins and Fresh Eyes and Miss Snark).

It's a thank-you to agents such as Donald Maass and editors such as Dave King and Rennie Browne who write books to share insights that help us become more successful and better writers.

It's a thank-you to the writers I've worked with in critique groups who have helped me with my own writing and in learning how to coach writers to strengthen story shortcomings.

And the biggest thank-you goes to my wife, Sarah, who has been a patient listener for, well, all the important times, and some not so consequential—the companion of my life.

It's harsh out there

Today's publishing climate is tougher than ever. To get an agent, your work has to stand out from hundreds and hundreds of submissions. For your agent to get you a book contract, your novel has to cut through hundreds more.

Your book has to be polished, diamond-sharp, and a rarity—you not only have to have professional-caliber writing and a great story, your novel needs to kick-start with compelling tension.

You only have seconds in an agent's hands

Established authors can ease into a story with description and mood (and even they aren't safe in the bookstore), but unpublished writers face a very different reality—agents suffering through heaps of submissions and looking for reasons to reject while at the same time hoping for a story worth reading.

On her blog, *Agent in the Middle,* 20-year veteran agent Lori Perkins said this:

> Your novel has to grab me by the first page, which is why we can reject you on one page.

> "I know most of what I need to know about a writer's chops in about a line and half."
>
> Dan Conaway, literary agent,
> Writers House

The odds are excellent that an agent will see all the reasons she needs for passing—or for reading more—on your first manuscript page. Just like agents and editors who see rivers of submissions, as a result of seeing hundreds of opening pages for novels, I can tell you that the first page typically foreshadows what's to come, story-wise and writing-wise. One quick skim usually provides all the reason I need to decide whether I will turn the page or decline the opportunity.

Often I see competent writing that fails to connect because the writer doesn't get what the novel's opening *must* do to hook a reader. Frequently I find a gripping opening pages later—too late. Most often a bog of exposition or backstory—what one writer calls "throat-clearing"—drags the story to a halt.

You still only have seconds on an editor's desk

Let's say you do land an agent, and the agent sends your story to an acquisitions editor. The same grim reality opens its maws—an audience of one with sharp, particular tastes who has an agenda that your story may or may not fit, who wants a great story but has a pile of submissions to go through, and for whom quickly finding a reason to pass is a good thing. One slip, and chomp, you're gone.

You still only have seconds at the bookstore

Okay, so your talent and work and luck pay off and your novel is published. Now it faces the cold, pragmatic reality of the bookstore. Sol Stein, a remarkable publisher/editor/author/playwright, writes in *Stein on Writing* of his observations in a bookstore.

"No [bookstore] browser went beyond page three. . ."

Sol Stein, publisher

In the fiction section, the most common pattern was for the browser to read the front flap of the book's jacket and then go to page one. No browser went beyond page three before either taking the book to the cashier or putting it down and picking up another to sample.

What did those readers see in the novels they chose to purchase, and what did they fail to see in the rejects?

You know.

Ask yourself what readers buy novels for. Is it. . .

➤ Lush descriptions?
➤ Great dialogue?
➤ Fascinating characters?
➤ Deep themes?

Nope. Just one thing.

Story

Those bookstore browsers—and the agent and editor before them—either saw signs of a story they wanted to read, or they did not. They either felt compelled to keep reading, or not. That quickly. You do it too, don't you?

It's not like when you ask a family member, or a friend, or even a critique group to read your new novel—they have to read your stuff.

No, in the real world, you have a page or two. And if it's that difficult with a bookstore browser who is on the hunt for a story to read, how tough do you think it is with a jaded, weary agent or a jaded, way-too-swamped acquisitions editor?

> "You can usually tell after a paragraph—a page, certainly—whether or not you're going to get hooked."
>
> Chuck Adams, Executive Editor
> Algonquin Books

To move your book toward the cash register. . .or generate a request by an agent for the full manuscript. . .or make it to an editorial meeting by an acquisitions editor. . .you need to kick-start your story, sentence by sentence, on your opening pages.

And then you have to keep pages turning

Beyond openings, this book tackles the art and craft that you need in order to focus every facet of your talent on compelling a reader to turn pages.

1: Storytelling

Coaching on the art of storytelling—motivating characters, creating tension, gripping your readers so they want to keep reading, and reading, and reading—so you get a feel for what your narrative must do to capture readers and to make the story live in their minds. Then come craft tools you'll utilize to make your story happen on the page.

2: Description

One of the most powerful, yet underutilized (or, sadly, sometimes over-utilized) tools for a novelist is description. I'll show you how to create description that not only describes, but characterizes. You'll write description that does far more than produce a simple snapshot of a scene or an action.

3: Dialogue

The other key tool for injecting life into your story is dialogue. You'll see how to craft dialogue that delivers the experience of a scene smoothly, clearly, and powerfully.

> "To hold our attention, a novel's action needs to compel us to read every word."
>
> Donald Maass, agent and author
> *Writing the Breakout Novel*

4: Technique

I'll illustrate a toolbox of craft techniques that include the all-important show/tell dichotomy and its impact on your story. I'll cover point of view, head-hopping, and flashbacks.

5: Words

How well you create a story experience in a reader's mind depends on the words you use—and don't use. Are adverbs truly *verboten*, or can they be your friend? What are the weak words that sap power from your narrative?

6: Workouts

Finally, you go to work applying the techniques and insights you've gained to real novel openings created by writers like you.

If this book does no more than guide you to focus on and to see the true effect and impact of your writing, it will have boosted you several rungs up the ladder to creating a publishable novel.

Last, but not least, I suggest you consider posting the definition below somewhere within sight at your place of writing.

> **com·pel**
> *verb*
> **a:** to force
> **b:** to urge irresistibly

Are you writing for effect?

If you want me to turn your pages, here's the effect I want your writing to have on me—I want it to trigger in me the sights and sounds and smells of what's happening. I don't want approximations, I want that *reality*. I want to experience the story, not just learn about what happens. And I want it to be effortless—I should be able to react without having to stop and think about the stimuli you put on a piece of paper. (That is not to say that good writing doesn't give you something to think about.)

Writing for effect is the core principle underlying my approach to creating an irresistible fiction narrative that immerses a reader in the experience of the story.

It's the lens through which I critique narrative in an edit and strive to view my own writing.

It's the objective that informs the coaching on storytelling, dialogue, description, and technique in this book.

It's knowing how to show and when to tell. It's why adverbs are often weak writing—and sometimes not.

It is the guiding light that can show you the way to a stronger story, and the searchlight that can illuminate shortcomings in your manuscript.

Failure to write for effect is why too many writers, especially beginning novelists, do little more than put information on the page and end up with little more than a report with a plot.

In storytelling, you're not writing to inform the reader—you deliver information, of course, but that's not the purpose—you're writing to **_affect_** the reader. To craft narrative that creates an **_effect_** in the reader's mind—the experience of the story.

Stimulus/response

Maybe it's the psychology major in me, but I can't help but think of the stimulus/response paradigm. Pavlov taught dogs to expect food when he rang a bell, and thereafter the dogs salivated at the sound of that bell.

You, the writer, produce a stimulus. The reader provides the response, imagining a scene or an action or an emotion. Actually, there's a reader element involved that a writer can't address—the reader's personal filters and baggage. A dog not trained to associate feeding with a bell won't salivate at the sound of one. For readers, as an elementary example, the word "cat" has a different effect on a cat lover than it does on a cat hater. You can't control that, but you can still load your narrative gun with the best possible ammo.

In practice, the workings of stimulus/response aren't simple, but they are the keys to writing for effect, and understanding that can open the door to successful storytelling.

You begin a story with a single stimulus—a word. Here's one now:

Vladimir's

Most words can't do much by themselves, so you string more words into a sentence that forms a different stimulus.

Vladimir's blade cut Johnson's throat, and Vladimir smiled.

Change one or two words, and the effect is different.

Vladimir's blade sliced open Johnson's throat, and Vladimir smiled.

To my mind, _sliced open_ is far more evocative than _cut_.

Another part of the effect here is to characterize Vladimir—for some reason, he enjoyed slicing open a man's throat. And this sentence raises story questions: Why did he slice the throat, and why did he smile? All that from just one sentence of nine words.

Although we're writing for effect, and the accumulating stimuli produce a dramatic portrayal of what's happening, it doesn't yet reach the level of delivering the experience of the story. The experience comes through the character.

Vladimir is the point-of-view character, but this narrative is objective so far, a camera's view. Novels provide a unique way to create an experience—*showing* what's happening in a character's mind.

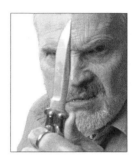

> Vladimir's blade sliced open Johnson's throat. The child-killer toppled, hands clutching his neck. Vladimir watched him writhe, and then become still. The bittersweet taste of vengeance filled Vladimir, and he smiled.

Your sentences accrue and, done well, coalesce into a greater stimulus—the story. The final result, the effect on your reader, begins with the word choices you make and how you put them together.

How you arrange words to affect your reader demands professional techniques aimed at maximizing the power of your narrative to create an experience for your reader. We'll dig into techniques that help you do just that.

Benchmark

At the end of this book are ten "workouts" where I ask you to apply the coaching herein to samples sent to me by writers. Below is one of the examples you'll be working on, the opening sixteen lines of a novel sent to me by an Australian writer (note the British punctuation).

To create a benchmark for changes in how you perceive a narrative after reading this book, I suggest you read this excerpt now, evaluate its strengths and shortcomings, and think about how you would edit it and/or what comments you would give the writer. Then carry on.

> 'Michael's gone!' Julia screamed into the payphone outside Flinders Street Train Station.
>
> 'Calm down, Mrs Stewart. She'll be with you shortly.'
>
> Julia bristled at the matter-of-factness of the receptionist's voice. 'I don't care if she's with the Queen. My husband is missing. I think I'm losing my mind.'
>
> 'Please hold and I'll see if I can interrupt.'
>
> Click. Mozart replaced the receptionist's voice. The familiar hold music from the past sounded surreal against the background tram and traffic noise of the Melbourne thoroughfare.
>
> A pedestrian bumped into her daughter's stroller, turning Shellie to tears.

'Stop that, you bad girl!' Julia rolled the stroller under the phone box, putting her child out of the way of the Friday afternoon commuters.

Shellie reached out and cried louder.

'Arrgghh!' Julia dropped the receiver, picked up the three year old and settled her on her hip. Shellie quieted, distracted now by an earring.

Ignoring her, Julia reached for the dangling receiver, and found silence. 'Hello? Hello!' *Don't be gone. I don't have any more change.*

'I thought I'd lost you.' The receptionist's cheerfulness was enough to piss off anyone.

> "I was at once impressed, delighted and amused. Your insights into the writing process are dead on!"
>
> Steven Gillis, *Walter Falls* and *The Weight of Nothing*

Section 1: Storytelling

Telling a story seems like a simple enough proposition: just set down what happens.

But to be a published novelist, telling your tale can't be what you'd do settin' on the porch and jawing about what happened to Uncle Abner back in '98, no sirree. It has to be compelling. (On the other hand, if we're talking about how Uncle Abner single-handedly defeated the attack of the space aliens. . .hmmmm.)

What makes a story compelling? How do you make it compelling? This first section takes up the story side of writing a novel, the thinking and planning and conceptualizing and imagining you have to do to reach a publishable level of story.

There are no magical answers, no one formula that you can input with characters and events that sums to a compelling story. This is an art, after all.

And there are no rules, either. If you do the opposite of everything advised in this book, but in doing so you create the experience of a compelling story, that's great.

No rules, no magical answers. . .but there are ways to think about how to craft what happens that create tension in your story, the necessary ingredient that forces readers to turn pages.

Storytelling

Story as river

A tale of two stories:

Enticed by a friend's recommendation, Ima Reader takes a seat in a punt on the shore of a gentle English river. The flat-bottom boat rocks a little, but she feels safe in the hands of Heezan Author, who stands ready at the stern, hands on the long pole used to push the boat. His photo on the back of the book was nice.

Heezan shoves off, and they glide down the river on an easy-going current. Heezan says, "Note the lovely hues of red and gold in the rose garden on the far bank." He steers the bow a few degrees toward the near shore. "And here is the poor peasant hut, its thatched roof more holes than not, where our hero was born, poor tyke, the sad victim of—"

"Oh, the hero. I'm so eager to see him." Ima leans forward and peers ahead.

"Soon enough, soon enough, Dear Reader. But first, see the ramshackle one-room schoolhouse where Hero first met Heroine, though their meeting was a tussle over who got the swing—"

Ima turns to Heezan. "Excuse me, sir…"

A sigh. "Yes?"

"Pull over to the bank, please."

"But there's so much story to be told."

The boat clunks against a dock and Ima steps out. "Too late." She gently closes the covers, never to return.

OR...

Feeling the pull of a fetching blurb, Ima Reader turns to page one and drops into a river raft. It races downstream, toward the roar of water churning over rocks. The raft noses around a bend, and ahead spray creates a mist above roiling water and granite boulders.

Sheezan Author, both hands with strangle-holds on the rudder at the rear, shouts, "I don't want to alarm you, but there are crocodiles between us and the end."

Ima grips a page. Her lips stretch in a grin of anticipation when she leans forward and says, "Let 'er rip!"

What if Ima Reader is an agent to whom you've just submitted a sample, and yours is the eleventy-eleventh submission she's opened that week?

Or an acquisitions editor at a publishing firm who wonders why in hell he agreed to look at your manuscript?

Or a bookstore browser deciding on what to buy for a weekend read (and your book is in that narrow window of only a few weeks to catch hold and create an audience)? These people turn to page one looking for one thing.

To be swept away.

And effortlessly, too. After all, the agent's tired, it's been a hard week, she's looked at dozens of crappy novels, and it's an act of will to tackle another one. The editor feels a migraine coming on, and the bookstore browser just had her transmission go out. Please, capture my mind and imagination and take me away from all this.

But how does a story do that? The story river readers want to ride races down mountain slopes, hurtles around sharp bends to reveal unexpected events, plunges into canyons and out again until a killer waterfall comes into view. Then it sweeps them over, they plunge and crash into the maelstrom of the story's climax, and then emerge into calm waters, safe and satisfied.

But how does an author sweep a reader along? The reader isn't in a craft pulled by a rope, nor propelled by oars or a motor. Instead, her imagination becomes one with the flow of the river.

What determines the nature of that flow? What lack makes it an easy-going stream, what element makes it a roller-coaster ride?

For a river, gravity furnishes passive power with inevitable pull. Where does the power of a story come from?

The gap

Screenwriter/story guru Robert McKee has a terrific way of thinking about what powers a story. Years back, I attended one of his intensive seminars on screenwriting, and I wish now I'd been ready to understand everything he had to offer. A brilliant screenwriter and story thinker, McKee nails what creates the ever-increasing rush of current in a story. In his book, *Story*, he calls it the "gap." While he writes primarily about screenwriting, he does talk about novels, and his insights are all about story, no matter what the form. This diagram from his book illustrates the gap.

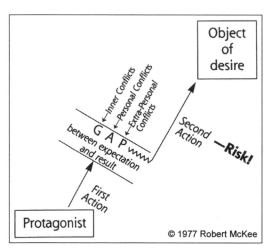

A character has an object of desire. That could be a treasure, a job, a person, catching a killer, anything. He takes action—risky action—to get it…but he doesn't succeed because of inner, personal, or external conflict. A gap opens between the character and his goal.

But he still wants what he wants—or, better, needs what he needs. So he takes a second action, one with greater risk. But again he is frustrated, and must try again. McKee says each effort should involve more risk; each time there should be more for the character to lose. Causes of the gap—the thing that stymies the protagonist—can even be things that seem pleasant, even the achievement of a similar goal…but underneath, like the current in the river, there's still that need that isn't satisfied.

So look at your story, especially the opening. Are you poling your reader down a lazy river, talking amiably about scenery and backstory? Or about to run the rapids only seconds after she boards?

The rapids don't, of course, have to be physical, as in an adventure story. They can be caused by internal conflict. They can be emotional, or interpersonal, or…hey, whatever your imagination desires.

A river is not all rapids

Your story river needs the tension of rapids and crocodiles to keep compelling readers forward, but keep in mind that a river, just as a story, needs eddies and calm pools, too. Without them, the traveler can be exhausted. Without them, the story cannot gather its energy for another run. Moments of calm serve to create more tension if your story has let the reader know—through your use of the gap—that all is not yet well.

But your river must still MOVE! When I write scenes and chapters, I don't consciously apply McKee's gap technique before writing. But my sense of that underlying mechanism is becoming more and more ingrained in me, more of the rudder that steers my characters deeper and deeper into complications.

Use the gap to give first aid to your story

"The gap" can be a terrific diagnostic tool. If your story feels lazy, or sags somewhere along the line, look at what is (and isn't) happening—does the character desire something, does he strive for it, is he blocked and forced to try again, to try something new at greater and greater risk?

Use "the gap" to help create irresistible pull for the river of your story.

"I found your kitty-cats in action hilarious as well as instructional, and I plan to share it with my critique group. Thanks so, so much for providing your insight."

Elaine Sims, *Unearthing Passions*

Start with kitty-cats in action

Opening your story *in medias res*, in the midst of something happening (versus placidly setting the scene), is key to engaging a reader. For example:

> Hairball raced across the clover, leaping honeybees, never taking his gaze from Barfie, praying that her grip would hold.

This opening raises immediate story questions that a reader will want to know the answers to—why is Hairball racing? Who is Barfie? *What* is Barfie? What do they have to do with each other? What's Barfie's scary-sounding problem?

Add unusual circumstances to action and you intensify interest. You've heard of "fish out of water" stories…how about "cat in water?"

> Up to his dewclaws in the cold wetness of the stream, Hairball wanted to yowl his discomfort, but he had to choke back all sound and focus on his prey.

Opening with action that confronts a character with a significant challenge will keep a reader moving down the page, too.

Hairball eyed the tree's towering height. It was an impossible climb. He was too small, too weak. But if he didn't climb, Barfie would fall to her death.

Plenty of story questions raised there. Now let's open with action combined with *jeopardy* for increased tension.

Barfie dug her claws into the branch, struggling to keep her balance. She dared not look down; her last glance at the dizzying height had almost sent her tumbling. Her ears caught a cracking sound...the branch was tearing away from the trunk.

Yeeks! A way to create even greater tension is to add *conflict* to action and jeopardy.

Hairball arched his back and hissed at the beast. It was three times his size, an alien species that crouched, poised to spring. There was no place to run. He extended his claws and braced himself. . .

Not all openings have to begin with physical action...but they MUST begin to raise story questions immediately. Remember that thoughts are action, too. Next we open with a character facing a different sort of jeopardy.

Hairball wondered if Barfie's spirit now rested on one of the puffy pillows in the sky, freed from her broken body. How would he face her mother after he'd sworn she would be safe?

Approaches you can use to kick-start your novel include:
- ➤ Start with something happening.
- ➤ Start with action in unusual circumstances.
- ➤ Open with action that challenges the character.
- ➤ Combine action with jeopardy for the character.
- ➤ Add conflict to action and jeopardy.

The point of all this is that your opening page narrative has to first be vivid enough to catch the reader's thoughts, and then compel reading further by raising story questions. I'll tell you something else—I think that for a new novelist to break in, the opening page of *every* chapter ought to do the same thing.

Storytelling
Tension in your first sentence

There's a reason for working to create tension with your very first sentence—it leads to the second sentence, and you draw your reader into your story sentence by sentence by sentence. It's clear that each sentence on the first page is charged with the responsibility to KEEP READERS MOVING FORWARD.

When you send a sample to an agent, or when an editor turns to your first page, you are on trial. Not just your work, but your ability. The agent/editor wants to know, can this writer engage me? Can this writer use language to *make* me read his story?

The story is on trial as well. You get a few hundred words to make your initial case that the journey through the next 80,000 words is worth it, and will reward your reader with a helluva reading experience.

And it all starts with that first line.

But there are so many things in your mind when you craft that first sentence—setting the scene, or characterizing, or creating action, or whatever—it's entirely possible to miss seeing a lack of tension.

Take me, for example. In one of my novels, I'd reworked that bloody first sentence scores of times, and it had evolved to this:

> "If you don't hook my attention and hold it in the first twenty-five to fifty words, you probably won't."
>
> Jim Hess
> writing competition judge

As I neared one of the bronze lions that guard the Chicago Art Institute, a lean man in a black overcoat aimed a small video camera at me.

While it did what I wanted it to in many ways, including setting the scene and starting with action, it nagged at me that something was missing.

Tension.

I realized that the problem—and the solution—lay in the verb. While "aimed" is descriptive enough, and it gives you a clear picture of the man's movement, it is otherwise lame. It describes the action, but doesn't characterize it in a way that can create tension. By the way, I think Stephen King is a master at creating mood and tension in this micro approach to word choice.

In this case, I needed to add a flavor that suggested something was amiss with this action, that there might be jeopardy attached. I didn't want to be as "on the nose" as something like "threatened." That wouldn't make a lot of sense, and would be ham-handed as well. I think the replacement verb below does the trick.

As I neared one of the bronze lions that guard the Chicago Art Institute, a lean man in a black overcoat targeted me with a small video camera.

For me, "targeted" adds an element of purpose to the man's action. And what do we do with targets? We hit them or shoot at them. That, it seems to me, is implicit in my choice of verb; my protagonist, Ailia, feels like a target, and that adds tension.

In addition, since we're in Ailia's point of view, this adds to characterization because it's her interpretation of the normally innocent action that lets the reader know that, for some reason, she sees it as a threat.

This is a tiny bit of writing for effect, true, but it contributes to the aggregate that delivers her experience.

After finding this soft spot in my own work, I decided to go through the many samples writers have sent to me and see how their first sentences fared in terms of creating some sense of tension. For example:

In the moment after midnight, the world held its breath.

For me, lots of tension there. Why did the world hold its breath? Why at midnight? What's happening? Here's another.

There's something there.

I like that one, too. There's menace in those three words, and I want to know more. A bit of dialogue opened the next sample.

"They're belly beads."

Hmm. Kinda interesting, but no hint of tension. In looking at the rest of the sample, there was no tension in the opening paragraphs. This writer will have to dig deeper.

Next, from a published novel, *Nectar from a Stone*, by Jane Guill.

Maelgwyn's "husbandly attention," as he called it, went on and on.

That opening line is packed with information and, for me, tension. In those eleven words I get the idea that sex is happening; that the recipient of Maelgwyn's attention doesn't think of it the same way that he does; and that she doesn't like it. This opening both establishes a relationship and smacks of the tension in it.

Here's another from a published work, E.B. White's *Charlotte's Web*.

"Where's Papa going with that ax?"

I defy anyone to not rush to the next sentence. Now back to some of the samples sent to me by unpublished writers.

Allison could sense something was wrong all the way to the roots of her fur.

There's tension alluded to here, but it doesn't grab me. I think it's the fact that I'm being told about the tension ("something was wrong") rather than being shown. I took another part of the opening paragraph and added it in this way:

Allison's father stepped into the doorway, and she tensed all the way to the roots of her fur.

21

That's a start at raising story questions and writing for effect. What about this one?

> Inspector Steve Masters of the National Security Branch watched her stride down the airport concourse.

Only the man's title and the "Security Branch" hint at tension, and vaguely. The lack lies in the action—just watching someone isn't tension-provoking. How about just a couple of tweaks. . .

> Inspector Steve Masters of the National Security Branch tracked his target through the airport concourse.

Another example:

> Grace stirred in bed, kept her eyes closed.

Nope. But a few sentences later, the writer had this:

> A floorboard creaked beneath the worn carpet.

Now, if that had been the first sentence, and then we had Grace stirring but keeping her eyes closed, I would wonder what Grace isn't seeing that makes the floor creak—there would be tension afoot. Next:

> Boccaha was a small fat balding man with bad teeth.

That simple description caused no tightening in my mind. For one thing, he's not doing anything, as far as we can see. As it happened in this sample, it took a couple of hundred words of exposition before anything actually happened.

Here's an opening (very long) sentence that focuses on scene.

> A crisp, bitter winter wind knifed between the buildings of downtown Seattle, slashing like transparent rapids through the alleys and streets, seeping into the cracks around doors and windows, and stealing under people's coats and hats as nature sought to balance hot and cold.

While I applaud the writer's effort to set the scene, and he has given thought to using active verbs, all we're really seeing is a windy day. No tension here. As it happened, his second paragraph started this way:

> Darren McAllister's stiffening body lay face-up in a green, rusted metal Dumpster, half-hidden by discarded pizza boxes and a bulging black plastic trash bag.

Okay, now you've got me. Add the wind in later, if you must, but give me tension to begin with. Interestingly, writers often have a real grabber of an opening sentence that comes later in the narrative.

Here's a writer who didn't wait around.

> She couldn't run any more, but she didn't dare stop.

Applause, applause. I want more. Guaranteed that I'll move on to the next sentence, and the writer increases her chances of hooking me. How about this one?

> The Reverend David Wilcox was walking slowly across the wet grass towards the rectory, where his friend Dr Alex Greer was waiting for him.

No sale. This was from a murder mystery. Not even enhancing the verbs ("walking slowly" needs help) would add edge to this simple movement. But about 1,200 words later in the story was this sentence:

> He lowered the pillow over Emily's face and pressed down firmly.

Now we're talking.

Go to the first line on your first page. If there's no tension, look for a way to add it—there's an agent or editor waiting to drop the blade like an executioner if he's not lured further into the story.

Six vital story ingredients

Okay, so what about that first page? What, in the 200 or so words that appear in the sixteen lines of narrative on your first page, can you do to propel a reader on? You can make sure your narrative has as many of these story elements as possible:

➤ Tension
➤ Story questions
➤ Voice
➤ Clarity
➤ Scene setting
➤ Character

There are more elements to a story, of course, and adequate grammar is a prerequisite, but these six are critical tools for engaging a reader, factors that can create the hook you need to reel in a weary agent or browsing reader.

Tension

"Tension on every page."

Donald Maass
literary agent

In discussions of writing craft, you hear about "tension" all the time. But what does that mean? Is it conflict on every page? Not necessarily. It means something in your narrative that creates a need in your reader, a small unease, an appetite to know more. It means that what happens in the story causes tension in the reader and fosters the lure of what will happen next. Tension is a real feeling that you, the reader, should experience on the *first* page of a novel. We're not talking breakout-in-a-sweat tension here, more like an itch-that-has-to-be-scratched version.

You don't have to have the main conflict in the first page of your novel to create tension. While it might be a stronger hook to begin with something like this . . .

> In ten seconds, the dirty bomb would contaminate Manhattan with enough radiation to make it a desert for fifty centuries.

. . . the tension element, as long as it comes from story questions that are meaningful to the reader, can be relatively mild compared to the overall conflict or jeopardy in the story. For example, the opening sentence from *Fly by Night* by Frances Hardinge:

> "But names are important!" the nursemaid protested.

There is implied conflict in that sentence, and story questions come tumbling out of it, certainly enough to carry you to the next sentence, and thus giving the writer a chance to sink in her claws.

But immediate conflict isn't the only way to create tension, although it's hard to beat as a hook-setter. Jeopardy, a sense of trouble ahead, can create enough tension to move the reader just enough further for more of the story to take hold. Here's the opening sentence from one of my manuscripts.

> Just after dark, death grabbed me by the tail.

Story questions

Perhaps my list should have started with story questions, for without them there would be no tension. You create story questions with information that forces a reader to wonder what will happen next (by information I mean action or dialogue in a scene). For example, how about this for the very first sentence you encounter in a novel?

> The spider crept onto Judy's bare neck.

Your knowledge of spiders raises instant questions: Will it bite Judy? Is it poisonous? Is it deadly? What will happen if she's bitten? Will she feel the spider and avoid the bite? *What's going to happen next?!*

Let's add a little more information and see what happens to the story questions.

> The black widow spider crept onto Judy's bare neck.

Uh-oh. Now you know it's poisonous, and its bite has more serious consequences—the stakes have been raised, the story question is intensified, and the tension mounts. And now you "see" the spider more clearly—it's black! Is that enough tension? Enough story questions? Maybe, but we can do better.

> The black widow spider crept onto Judy's bare neck. She stirred in her sleep.

She's asleep? Ohmygod! New story question: will she wake up in time to deal with the spider? Once more:

> The black widow spider crept onto Judy's bare neck. She stirred in her sleep. A second black widow crawled onto her naked skin.

New story questions (and tension): How many black widows are there? Where is she that there are so many? *What will happen next?!* And we did this with only three sentences. Just for fun, what if this comes next?

> Judy opened her eyes just as the first spider crawled onto her cheek. She looked down to see what tickled, and then she grinned.

How's that for a story-question-raiser?

Voice

What the heck is "voice?" Here's a definition adapted from a most excellent book, *Self-editing for Fiction Writers:* "it is the way sentences read as prose." I would add this: how they sound in your head.

In fiction, there are two basic voices: that of the author, and that of a character. In this book, the voice you read/hear is mine. I can cut loose and do what I want, unrestricted by theme or venue or a character. *I'm* the character.

In fiction written from the omniscient point of view, the voice is the author's. When well done, as with authors such as John Irving, an author's voice can succeed in engaging the reader. Here's the opening from Irving's *The Fourth Hand*:

Imagine a young man on his way to a less-than-thirty-second event—the loss of his left hand, long before he reached middle age.

As a schoolboy, he was a promising student, a fair-minded and likable kid, without being terribly original. Those classmates who could remember the future hand recipient from his elementary-school days would never have described him as daring. Later, in high school, his success with girls notwithstanding, he was rarely a bold boy, certainly not a reckless one. While he was irrefutably good-looking, what his former girlfriends would recall as most appealing about him was that he deferred to them.

The other voices you hear in fiction are those of the characters. For my money, that includes description of action and setting within a particular character's narrative. Everything should evoke a sense of character. In a close third-person point of view, I think the author should suppress his own voice and bring out that of the character. I frequently see instances where a narrative that's supposed to be that of a child is robbed of authenticity by word choices in the descriptive elements that are clearly adult in nature.

To exemplify, here's how the narratives of three very different characters describe the same incident, falling off a bicycle:

A five-year-old boy:

The front wheel hit a rock and he hit the ground hard. He skinned his knee and it bled a lot. His mom was gonna be mad about the rip in his pants.

A teenage boy:

The front wheel banged into a big freakin' rock and the handlebars ripped out of his hands. He flew off the bike and crashed. The pavement trashed his jeans and skinned his knee, which bled like a stuck pig. It hurt like hell, and Jenny wasn't going to want to go to the movie with him looking like this.

A middle-aged college professor:

The front wheel struck a large rock and the handlebars twisted from his grasp. He plunged over the falling bicycle and slammed into the asphalt road. Like sandpaper, the black, gritty surface tore open his jeans and scraped skin from his kneecap. It bled furiously and he cursed the rock, hoping he hadn't fractured the knee.

I've read that a number of agents profess that voice is the thing they respond to most in a submission. Literary agent Andrea Somberg says this:

Every manuscript I take on is distinctive in its own right, but each of them has one thing in common: an engaging narrative voice. By this I mean a writing style that pulls me in and makes me feel like I'm a part of the story and the characters' lives.

Voice is the one thing that can suck you into a story even without initial tension and story questions (though those requirements cannot be avoided for long).

Perhaps it's easier to think about what voice does rather than what it is. Here are some characteristics of a voice that will lead a reader on:

➤ **Freshness.** It "sounds" fresh in the reader's mind. The language is not mundane, but flavored. The ideas evoked are out of the ordinary. The way things are put is uncommon. Words that create a distinct sense of "personality" is another way to think of this aspect of voice.

➤ **Confidence.** A strong voice immediately says to a reader, "You can trust me. I know a terrific story, and you can relax and enjoy because I know how to tell it so well that it becomes an experience in your mind." John Irving's voice has that confidence.

➤ **Lucidity.** A clear voice that slips scenes and sights and sounds easily into your mind, with no struggle to comprehend or follow, can sweep you swiftly into the current of a story.

By the way, as an editor, I work hard to respect and preserve a writer's voice. It would be too easy to rewrite so that it "sounds" better to me. As a result, you may see examples in this book where you don't care for the voice all that much. Me neither, but the writer has to have a chance to try it out.

Clarity

Maybe the need for this story element on your first page seems obvious, but it can be harder to achieve than you think. Take this opening sentence from one of my workshoppers:

> Mark Johnson's daughter had disappeared, and that was all that mattered to him.

What could have been an intriguing opening was, for me, diminished by what it fails to make clear: What is the relationship between the missing girl and the point-of-view character, the "him?" Is she Mark Johnson's daughter? Because the pronoun "him" in first sentence is unclear as to whom it refers, the disappearing daughter could be an as-yet-unnamed protagonist's, that of a friend, or boss, or a crime victim. Yes, we know that the girl matters to "him," and we might assume that she's his daughter, but it isn't clear.

Even if you simply reverse the positions of the pronoun and the name, it works better for me.

> His daughter had disappeared, and that was all that mattered to Mark Johnson.

Here's another example; this description is from the point of view of someone inside an airplane.

> In the distance, the ice-capped peaks of the Rockies rose intermittently among the clouds. Far above the peaks, the roar of the airplane pierced the shrieking winds of the atmosphere.

The dissonance here, for me, was that in the first sentence the peaks are in the distance and in the second, the airplane is above them. Isn't the following more clear?

> The ice-capped peaks of the Rockies rose intermittently among the clouds. High above them, the roar of the airplane pierced the shrieking winds of the atmosphere.

Scene-setting

One of the most damaging flaws I see in manuscripts is failure to set the scene effectively—or at all. Some are more like radio scripts than novels.

Others are simply underdone, probably because the writer puts down a sparse description that evokes the whole picture in his mind but fails to get it in on paper.

Why is that a problem? Primarily because, although readers bring their imaginations to your novel and willingly take part in fleshing out the vision, they need to experience characters and action in *context*. It helps a reader to slip into the shoes of a character if she knows whether the shoes are walking along a snow-covered sidewalk or wading a stream. I'll illustrate. First, a snippet of dialogue.

> Roger said, "Don't you think that's a bit skimpy?"
> Maggie twirled. "You don't like it?"

Context can give meaning. I'll put these players into two different contexts to show how the meaning of their dialogue is affected.

> Roger opened the dressing room door and found Maggie admiring herself in a full-length mirror. He stepped inside and shut the door on the caterwauling of the woman currently on stage. Even though Maggie was the next to perform, she didn't seem nervous at all. Roger said, "Don't you think that's a bit skimpy?"
> Maggie twirled. "You don't like it?"

Okay, same dialogue, different context.

> The window rattled with the impact of the Arctic Express that had struck the city that morning. Roger pulled on his parka and then scraped frost off the glass to peer into the swirling snow outside. He turned to find Maggie waiting at the front door. Roger said, "Don't you think that's a bit skimpy?"
> Maggie twirled. "You don't like it?"

We don't yet know what Maggie is wearing, but we do know that in the first situation Roger doesn't think she should go out in front of an audience with that little on. In this context, the subtext is that Roger is possessive and jealous, and his concern is about losing Maggie because she's so attractive to others.

In the second example, he doesn't think she's sufficiently protected against a dangerous storm. The context leads us to think of Roger as a caring man who is concerned about Maggie's well-being.

In each case, where the scene is set, and how the environment in which these characters act impacts them, give context to the character's actions and words. Context can effortlessly give the reader an understanding—even better, a feeling—for what's happening. And in these examples, context tells us that that conflict is just about to blossom. Ahhh, tension.

Please, set the scene early on, within the context of action, so that when you get to who the reader knows what and where.

Character

While plot is a tool to engage and entertain a reader, it is character that makes them come to care about what happens, and it is character that invests meaning into what happens. Take every chance you have to add to the characterization of your protagonist—or antagonist—to more deeply engage your reader. And that requires action.

You know the old saw, "Do as I say, not as I do." The truth in this cliché is that character derives from action, not words. If a politician says he wants an honorable campaign that focuses on issues, but his campaign spews slur after slur at his opponent, then which is the true reflection of the politician's character?

Words can lie. Fiction sometimes uses the literary device of an "unreliable narrator" in which the credibility of the teller of the story is compromised. The character of an unreliable narrator comes from both what he does and the contrast with what he says. Behavior (action) is character.

More than that, the events of a story—plot—should spring from character, not simply be things that happen to him. It is what a character decides to do that should create events. For a simple example, let's consider a boy on his first day at a new school.

> Ron strolled past the gym at recess. It was his first day in seventh grade, and he didn't know anyone at this school. He hated moving.
>
> But there had been a nice moment in English class. The teacher had just started when a girl rushed in right after the bell. She looked for a place to sit, but all the desks were taken.
>
> He didn't know why, but he had stood, picked up his books, and gestured her to his seat.

The smile she had given him—and she was a very pretty girl—had just about wiped out what the teacher had said for the rest of the class.

A deep voice came from his left. "Hey, goody two-shoes."

Three boys lounged on a porch at the side of the gym. The big one looked like a man. He even had a mustache. That one said, "Why'd you give Carol your seat?" The "goody two-shoes" had come from him.

Ron shrugged.

The big kid swaggered over to Ron and scowled down. "We don't do that chickenshit stuff here."

Ron had to look up; God, the boy was big. Fighting words. Coming from a monster.

Ron's first choice of action, in the classroom, revealed a facet of character, and has led to conflict with a really big, nasty guy. Ron's next action will reveal character at a deep level. If he keeps his mouth shut, or maybe even runs, he's a coward. In this case, here's what Ron did:

Ron gazed straight into the boy/man's eyes and said, "Well, where I come from, it's what a gentleman does." Then he had to look away. He stepped around the big guy and walked, every muscle in his back tensed.

The 7th vital element: craft

When you're submitting your novel to an agent or an editor, there's one other element you absolutely must have: professional-level craft. Their minds are honed to sharply critical instruments that are on the lookout for soft spots in your narrative, and every little glitch or weakness counts against you.

After reading hudreds of submissions to my editing service and blog, I've come to react very quickly to signs of less-than-professional writing craft, and they are a major turn-off. Things that LEAP out at me:

➢ Overuse of adverbs and adjectives
➢ Weak verbs
➢ Comma faults (usually missing commas)

In addition to the six elements I've talked about, you need to have:

➢ Correct grammar and spelling—if you're not good at this, pay a copy editor to go through your manuscript
➢ Crisp, tight, lean writing
➢ No clichés

The professional audience you'll face is the reason that this book not only coaches you on story, but on craft as well.

Storytelling

The inciting incident: story launch pad

Every good story is launched by an "inciting incident." But does it have to be on page one? In surfing the Web I came across advice in one place to make it happen at the opening of your story, and in another place to have it occur as soon as possible after the story opens. I think that's mostly right, but not altogether. First, just exactly what is an inciting incident?

Robert McKee, in his excellent book, *Story*, defines it this way:

> An event that radically upsets the balance of forces in the protagonist's life.

So when must the inciting event occur? Well, there's no imbalance created unless the reader has some idea of the life the protagonist currently knows. If you can find a way to make it happen within a paragraph or two of the opening of your story, I think that's a smart thing to do. However, it can happen later—but only if there are other story elements that propel the reader along the stream of your narrative.

McKee cites the film *Rocky* as an example of a delayed inciting incident. He figures the true inciting event is where Rocky is invited to fight the world champion. But that doesn't happen until a half hour into the film. Until then, the story that keeps the audience involved is the developing love story between Rocky and Adrian.

Wherever the inciting incident occurs, what precedes it must have tension, must be raising story questions that keep the reader involved. It can't just be exposition that lays out the protagonist's life.

A question rises in my mind from McKee's definition: How much does a reader first have to understand about the protagonist's life to give the imbalance meaning? I often see manuscripts in which the effort to do this leads to gobs of exposition that stop the story cold. In *Rocky,* the film takes a long time to first create Rocky's life. But keep in mind that a theater audience is a captive audience.

The answer lies in the nature of the incident. For a crime victim who is stabbed or shot, the imbalance is immediate and clear. In a literary novel, it might be much more subtle.

Now that I think about it, I wonder if Rocky meeting Adrian isn't the real inciting incident—would he have accepted the fight challenge if he and his life hadn't already been substantially changed by falling in love?

Another way to look at understanding the inciting incident is to key in on the word "provoke."

> An event that provokes a desire in the protagonist that he is compelled to satisfy.

"Compelled" is the key. If he can say forget about it, it's not much of a desire, is it? Here's another one:

> An event that forces a character to take action in pursuit of something he needs.

McKee would argue that a protagonist's desire is to bring her life back into balance. That makes sense to me, but it seems too abstract. Specifically, what is the nature of this incident?

It can be negative (and, it seems, usually is).
- ➤ The banker's children are kidnapped.
- ➤ An innocent woman is accused of a hideous crime.
- ➤ A young mother is fired from her job.

> An event that provokes a desire in the protagonist that he is *compelled* to satisfy.

The event can be positive, too, but so hugely positive that it unbalances things and can throw a life out of balance and create new desires.
- ➤ Rocky is invited to fight the champ.
- ➤ A grocery clerk wins the lottery.
- ➤ A secretary is promoted over her boss.

> A battered woman escapes to a shelter.
> A man in a happy relationship is smitten by a beautiful woman.

I think McKee's notion that the inciting event throws a protagonist's life out of balance is a good one. Anything out of balance is bound to create tension and conflict—will it fall? Will it right itself? The main result of the event, to create a desire in the character to regain balance, is the fuel that fires the engine of your story.

In McKee's scheme of things, your protagonist must have a powerful desire. He must then attempt to satisfy it. But his attempt is frustrated. He fails to achieve it because of something the antagonist does (preferably), or perhaps something the protagonist fails to do, or some other story element.

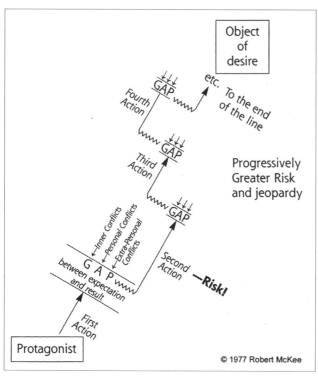

Your story picks up momentum and tension at this point because the character has to try again and, because of the nature of his failure and his desire, has to take a risk. A risk with negative consequences. Yep, he fails again. The negative consequences raise the stakes. He has to try again, and this time take an even greater risk. With greater consequences. He fails again. And so on.

For example, in a historical novel, let's say the daughter of a king is sent to live with the neighboring king in the age-old tradition of fostering. This upsets the balance of her happy life at home, but the consequences are potentially positive, and she makes no effort to change things. This isn't an inciting incident because, even though the balance of her life is disturbed, there's no jeopardy attached.

Then, on the journey to the neighboring kingdom, her party is attacked. She is taken and sold as a slave to another kingdom. Now *that's* an inciting incident. Her desire is to return to the life she knew, and there's the risk of being beaten, raped, or killed if she tries to escape. But try she must, because her life as a slave is a horror to her.

You can write the story from there.

> "Fiction is about trouble. Trouble is a direct consequence of desire. Characters are living embodiments of desire. A character in need is the force that sets a story in motion."
>
> Rick DeMarinis
> *The Art & Craft of the Short Story*

Storytelling
An engine named desire

During a Winter Olympics race, an American speed-skater was knocked down by a competitor who fell. The American slid blades-first into the side barrier, on her back, clearly out of the race.

But even before she'd stopped slamming into the barrier she was scrambling to regain her feet. The instant she was upright, her entire focus went down the ice. The intensity in her eyes and the set of her mouth were almost palpable, even on a television screen. She took off, her desire still powerful, her determination everything, and my heart and admiration went out to her. I was rooting for her. And respecting her. And liking her.

If you can get a reader feeling that way about your character, you're on your way to compelling storytelling. So how do you do that?

With desire.

Screenwriting guru Robert McKee says that a story's inciting incident is an event that radically upsets the balance of forces in the character's life. But to what end?

He goes on to say that the character must react to the event, otherwise there would be no story. But react with what?

A desire. A goal to be achieved. The high-octane fuel that gives your story power.

In McKee's approach, the desire is for the character to put his/her life back into balance. Let's say a character's children have been kidnapped. Of course the character doesn't think, "Dang, my life is out of balance. My desire is to regain my balance." No, the desire would be a specific goal, to get his children back from the kidnappers.

Is this right, then? A desire? Another craft instruction book tells us that fiction is about trouble. And we've all heard the cliché: get your character up a tree and throw rocks at him until he figures out how to get down.

But the "trouble" model is a passive one. Oh, there should be trouble, but it needs to come as a result of what characters do. Because they have a desire. Because they take risks in striving to achieve their desire.

It's this pursuit of a desire that creates the "rooting factor" that draws readers into a story, that gives them something to identify and empathize with. Just as I did that Olympic skater.

The "strive" is the thing. Without it, your sleek vehicle of a novel has no gas in its tank. One of my editing clients was a good writer. He'd done his research well, the language was good. He'd created a pleasant, likeable character. Smart. Pretty. Decent.

Abandoned, alone, Shedder *had* to catch the mouse.

But the character just drifted through her life, reacting to things, never initiating much, not striving. There was no tension. Nothing compelling me to turn the page. My recommendation was to create a strong inciting incident at the front of the story, to knock the character far out of her happy life.

Why isn't a happy story good enough? Why is it a good idea to trouble our characters, knock them down, and then keep knocking them down as they struggle? Why does that make them more compelling, more watchable?

Because, as human beings, we struggle too. In our ordinary lives, we may struggle with things small or large, but struggle we must. We understand how a character feels who has been knocked down. And here's the thing that a novel can do that lifts it from being mere entertainment: show us something about how to be a human being.

Learning to be a human being has a lifelong learning curve, and we can use all the help we can get because there aren't many good instruction books. Although novels are fiction, they can instruct us on the truths of being human.

Fiction models behavior for us, teaches us what (in the writer's imagination) works, and what doesn't work. We like to see characters desire and yearn and attempt because it helps us understand, maybe, what we can do in our own lives.

In thinking about my first novel after coming across McKee's idea of creating a desire in a character, I thought I'd failed to do that in my main protagonist: it seemed to me that he mostly reacted to events.

But then I realized that, unwittingly, I'd done one of the things McKee talks about: created an *unconscious* desire. My character's inciting event really pulled the rug out from under his life, but on the surface he seemed satisfied with the way things were. He just wanted, it seemed, to keep on doing his work. But unconsciously, it was the opposite.

My job as a writer is to learn to do it wittingly.

McKee says that **a story is more powerful if a character has an unconscious desire that works in opposition to the conscious desire.**

This is heady stuff for a simple guy like me, but I think I see how it can work. For example, let's say a man's wife is kidnapped and a ransom is demanded. His surface desire is to rescue her. That's what society, his friends, his peers, and he himself expects. Standard thriller stuff, you've seen it a thousand times.

But what if he hates his wife? Then his unconscious desire, the one that can't be admitted out loud, is to somehow lose her. This may remind you of the plot of the film *Ruthless People,* only Danny DeVito's desire to get rid of Bette Midler, his wife, is far from unconscious.

In my novel, darned if my protagonist's unconscious desire didn't affect what happened when he pursued conscious goals. Eventually his conscious goal came to be the same as the unconscious one, and he grew.

Checklist for your narrative:

> ➤ Does it contain an inciting incident that throws your protagonist's life severely out of balance? (By the way, your antagonist might need an inciting incident, too, such as the opposition of the protagonist.)
> ➤ Does the event create a conscious desire in your character?
> ➤ Does your reader know about it?
> ➤ Does your character immediately take action, take a risk to achieve a goal that springs from the inciting event?
> ➤ Optional: Does it create an unconscious, contrary desire?

These are the elements that not only create the engine that will drive your story, they create the fuel. The horsepower of that engine, and its power to affect the reader, depend on:

> ➤ How severely your character's life is thrown for a loop, i.e., how damaging are the consequences, how high the stakes?
> ➤ The difficulty of achieving the desire that is aroused
> ➤ The size of the risks she must take to recover

Storytelling

Four ways to create tension

We all have plenty of tension in our lives, so why on earth would we ask—no, *demand* more? Because it feels good in a page-turner story. What happens when you don't deliver a simmering dollop of tension on virtually every page of your novel manuscript?

The agent mails a rejection.

The acquisitions editor says, "Pass."

Agents and editors all *want* to discover an outstanding story. They want to be *compelled* to turn your pages. But they see so many hundreds of submissions that your storytelling needs to be almost perfectly irresistible to get them to go much beyond page one.

Tension doesn't have to come from bloody, balls-to-the-wall action; it can be torment inside a character's head, or a verbal duel in a courtroom, or delivering the diagnosis in a doctor's office.

Nor does it have to come entirely from the main conflict in your story. Donald Maass talks about using bridging conflict when you're not focused on the main pain.

Continuous microtension

Thriller writer Tess Gerritsen wrote in her blog about a talk by Donald Maass and hearing about his notion of "continuous microtension." In a story with a high level of conflict, she says, there's ". . .an underlying sense that something important is always about to happen, or could happen."

Tess added her take on the technique.

> Microtension is that sense that, on every page of the novel, there's conflict in the air, or that characters are slightly off-balance. It needn't be a flat-out argument or a gun battle or a huge confrontation. In fact, you can't throw in too many major conflicts or what you'll get is melodrama. But small and continuous doses of tension keep the story moving and keep the pages turning.

Frustrate your character

In a critique group member's novel, she created a simple but effective bit of tension during a question-and-answer session at a public meeting. The protagonist raises her hand to ask a question. Someone else is called on. She lowers her hand. She tries this a couple more times, but is still not called upon. She feels frustration, and her own tension builds. Finally, after being passed over yet again, she decides to just leave her hand in the air. The reader thinks that surely this will succeed. She's ignored again. Finally she waves her hand and gets to ask her question. So, while the main tension in the scene was building at a slower rate, there was still pressure.

Add character spin to create tension

The way the doc in this cartoon spins the facts reveals his bias and agenda. Every few years, a political season inundates us with politicians spinning each other's words and positions in order to distort and contrast them. I once hated the idea of spin…until it occurred to me that spin is a terrific way to create drama in a story. Spin comes from agendas, the *intentions* of characters. When characters want something in every scene and words and actions are guided by conflicting agendas, you automatically generate tension, and characters boil with action and dialogue.

Sol Stein, in *Stein on Writing*, uses the idea of agendas as "scripts" when he talks about the Actors Studio method for developing drama.

For example, let's say Faith, a compulsive gambler, is accused of murdering a sleazy bookmaker. Best friend Percy believes that Faith can do no wrong. Daggett, the district attorney, believes Faith is a liar who will do anything to get rid of a staggering debt to the bookmaker. On the surface, Percy and Daggett share a goal: to learn the truth. But differences in their internal views and agendas spin what they think, say, and do…

Percy screeches his car to a halt in front of the brownstone. Faith had sounded frightened and desperate when she called. Rushing from his car, he finds her being led out the front door by the district attorney, Daggett.

Faith's dress hangs in tatters and a bruise swells on her cheek. She staggers, and Percy races up the steps to steady her. Holding one arm as Daggett holds the other, Percy says, "My God. He tried to kill you!"

Daggett shakes his head. "That's what she hopes we'll think." He wrenches Faith's arms behind her back and hobbles her wrists with handcuffs.

Poor Faith. Spin also applies to how characters interpret information. On the political side, your orientation will add spin to the words "embryonic stem-cell research" that turns them into anathema, nirvana, or something in between. The same goes for your characters. And if two characters have different agendas, think what that can mean.

Percy believes Faith is innocent and wants to protect her, Daggett believes she's guilty down to the marrow of her bones and wants to convict her. So here's how those two characters spin the same input.

Faith's determined expression wavers, then breaks. "I'm guilty. I did it."

Percy shakes his head. She must be covering for someone. "How can you say that, Faith?" He glances at Daggett, who wears a smile that reminds him of a bear trap.

Daggett says, "Because she's guilty, guilty, guilty."

Clearly, agendas that are at cross-purposes spin up terrific tension. So ask each character in a scene these two questions:
1. What's your agenda in this situation?
2. What do you believe the other character's agenda is?

Then let 'em duke it out…and don't let either of them win, at least not for a few chapters.

Unsettle happy scenes with future jeopardy

Writer/agent Donald Maass writes of a need for tension on every page. *Every* page? Can't a character have a happy time now and then? Not really, at least not unmitigated happiness, not if you want to compel. If there isn't trouble in a scene, the reader must anticipate trouble to come.

The ironic humor in the cartoon comes from the reader knowing about danger ahead that the characters don't.

In a narrative, you can build tension the same way, by giving the reader knowledge about danger ahead that the protagonist doesn't have.

For example, here's an innocent-seeming scene:

> Steve gunned the engine and the boat surged forward. Laura rose from the water on her skis, unsteady at first, but gaining control. She was able to give him a quick wave and a big smile.
>
> Steve started a turn that would take her near the dam, where the lake plunged into the canyon below. Spray cooled her sun-warm skin and the speed thrilled. The force of the turn sent her arcing out behind the boat, swinging wide toward the spillway and gaining speed.
>
> She couldn't have been more alive, nor more in love.

Everything sounds loverly, but what if the writer has previously planted this:

> Steve is a serial killer who romances women and then kills them, and water is always an element in his *modus operandi*.

Because of this foreknowledge, the reader will feel tension from the moment Laura gets into that boat, and it will only build. Is she headed over the lip of that dam? You could call this a slow-burning fuse of continuous microtension. You plant a bomb, light the fuse, and then carry on with the reader tensing for the explosion. You put it off. . .and off. . .and off. . .

You don't have to create overt conflict on every page—a story with strong stakes and consequences makes it possible to use *impending* conflict to keep building tension in a reader. **There will be tension on every page even without direct conflict.** Have those happy moments, but create "when-will-the-trouble-I-know-is-coming-strike?" story questions that foreshadow trouble which will damage or diminish the protagonist.

> "Maybe I will care about her. But I don't. And I *need that to want to keep reading about her*."
>
> a critique partner

Storytelling
Creating the care factor

Readers demand a protagonist that they can care about. Not necessarily like, but care about. Uber-fiction-agent Donald Maass, in his *Writing the Breakout Novel* book and workbook, tells us that one key characteristic of the 100 bestselling novels that he analyzed is that the authors created protagonists that readers cared about.

Thus it comes to pass that acquisitions editors at publishing houses demand that your manuscript and mine have that characteristic. But how do you make it happen?

Relationships

Lou Aronica, an editor and the publisher of scores of best-selling novels, told me that the number one way to create caring for a character is to show the character in a relationship. This is not, he stressed, to make a reader *like* a character, but to create empathy, a person-to-person connection that can cause a reader to care about what happens to a character, even one that is otherwise not appealing. We all have relationships, and experiencing one on the page makes the character more "like us." I read a novel in which the protagonist was a pedophile and killer, and while the character was disgusting in many ways, there were sides of him with which I empathized.

Here's just such a character: Born-Again Bobby Strunk, who when you meet him, is an obese, slovenly, crude, arrogant, corrupt religious leader. Yet by the end of the novel, you care about him. The caring begins with this:

He rounded a curve and the wrought-iron gate at the Shady Farms entrance hung open before him. Residents were unlikely to run away. The Farms was their haven; they had no desire to leave, except on field trips into town for a movie or an ice cream treat. Bobby drove between rows of tall oaks with overarching branches that formed a leafy roof over the driveway.

He parked in front of the converted plantation mansion. Six three-story pillars graced the white Greek Revival structure. A thirty-foot magnolia tree littered the lawn with fallen pink blossoms. Bobby regretted leaving the air-conditioned comfort of his black Lincoln to crunch across the gravel parking lot to the main entrance.

Inside, ceiling fans moved the humidity around but created no relief. He wrinkled his nose at the aromas of mold and the ammonia the janitor used to try to get rid of it.

Sister Mary Agnes, stout in her black habit, came down a sweeping double staircase to greet him. Her somber clothing contrasted sharply with the mansion's high-ceilinged elegance, but the nun always seemed at home. Smile lines crinkling the corners of her blue eyes, she said, "Reverend Strunk, so good to see you. Sadie will be delighted."

Bobby thought Catholics had a crazy religion, what with their Latin nobody could understand and a mutilated Christ pinned to the cross. But integrity and devotion radiated from this woman, and that was what he wanted for his little sister. "How is she?"

"Just as healthy and happy as ever. I think she's out on the shuffleboard court with a couple of our teenagers."

Bobby found Sadie crowing and clapping her chubby hands at knocking her opponent's puck off the ten-spot.

He called out, "Little sister."

She spun, and when she saw him a huge smile glowed. She ran to him, her clumsy gait typical of the short-legged, heavy body of Down Syndrome. Sadie threw herself at Bobby with arms open for a huge hug. He returned it with equal vigor. Comforted and rewarded by her unconditional love, his troubles left him.

Bobby left behind all thoughts of being the man liberals labeled "the leader of the nation's most volatile right-wing

Christian sect." He was a big brother, happily spending the next five hours with his twenty-year-old little sister, pushing her in the swing, laughing on the teeter-totter, dancing, and playing go fish.

They danced the Twist to '50s rock and roll in the rec room. They ate hot dogs and potato salad on the lawn, and talked about her world, a safe place with caregivers always at hand, classes to help her learn, and activities to engage her.

Even dead people count

A story opens with the protagonist deep in an emotional fugue—he doesn't really feel anything. And he's a gun for hire, able to kill with only a minor (and key) qualm. The reasons for his fugue are mysterious, and they need to stay that way for at least half of the novel.

So how can a reader feel empathy for a character that feels nothing? Through a relationship that both establishes the mystery and tugs at the reader just enough to understand the troubled nature of the man. From the chapter that introduces him:

> Jake Black pulled the trigger again.
>
> Again the woman staggered. Then she dove off the flat rooftop after the little girl, her muffled laughter falling away.
>
> A nasty mechanical buzz blasted him—his alarm clock yelling at him. He groped and turned it off, then realized that he was holding his breath, his jaws clenched and aching.
>
> Why?
>
> As he did every morning, he turned to a snapshot in a plain black frame on his nightstand—Amy, forever five years old, in her favorite, flowery party dress. He touched the tiny silver crucifix hanging by its chain from a corner of the frame. Amy wore it in the picture.
>
> Why could he see her face in the photo but not in his memory? The crucifix glittered, and then he couldn't look at it any more.
>
> In the bathroom, his red, puffy eyes stared at him from the medicine-cabinet mirror. He wondered about the moisture on his cheeks. More and more, he found it there when he woke. He touched it with a fingertip, then tasted. Salty.

Another care factor: passion

Aronica told me that a second trait that can create a caring connection with a character is passion for achieving something. People driven to achieve, or fighting for a cause bigger than themselves, is something we can admire, and that brings the character closer to us. "Passion" is a facet of the "desire" I've talked about.

In the film *Rocky*, his passion for making the best of himself for the big fight takes him and the audience through rigorous training. The audience works with him every bit of the way, and then celebrates with him when he makes his triumphal run up the steps.

In Ayn Rand's *The Fountainhead*, Howard Roark's passion for his design and for his vision of what it could be even in the face of crushing opposition create a huge "rooting factor."

This is one that can work with both protagonists and antagonists. In the film, *Spider-Man 2*, Doctor Octopus has a goal of achieving a new energy source, which is admirable. Unfortunately, he goes a little nuts about it and does bad things to get there, but his fundamental passion is positive, and that keeps a human core alive inside him, and we can care about him when he sacrifices his life to save the city.

Lastly, caring about others

Showing a character caring is perhaps a form of having a relationship, but I think it's distinct enough to point out. Here's an example of putting that to work for an antagonist.

Wait, an antagonist? The bad guy? Caring? You bet. Sure, you can have a purely evil villain, and readers can enjoy the ride. But a novel has more depth and dimension when the antagonist is also seen as human by the reader. If a reader has just a little bit of connection with the opposition, then the lessons of how not to be a human being are more valid, and valuable.

So, if you can create connections between your reader and your antagonist, the story has set another hook, and the reader is drawn in more deeply.

Here's an illustration of caring. When we first meet Drago, we don't have a clue that he will eventually do very bad things. It would be nice for the reader to be on his side, even if only a little bit, so his arc into evil will be greater and more meaningful. Here's how we meet Drago:

> The percussive *whup-whup-whup* of a helicopter drew Drago to a porthole in his galleon's quarterdeck cabin. In the forest clearing where his ship and two others of his clan rested, a half-dozen clan children, teens to toddlers, built a

snowman. The tall curved hulls of the sixteenth-century Spanish vessels, all grace when they sailed through the air, now seemed awkward, supports angling out like spider legs to hold them upright. The daylight was dim under the gray January sky, but that didn't seem to matter to the children.

The helicopter grew closer and smothered their giggles. The galleons vanished behind *glaméres* of snow-clad forest, the illusions broadcast by alert sentries.

All save one of the children disappeared as well, disguised as young trees. Little Alexandra, her skills not yet awakened, burst into tears. Drago swung the porthole open to help her with a concealing *glamére*, but then a sapling scooped up the child. In the flicker of a thought, a fat squirrel appeared in her place. Satisfied, he closed the port against the chill.

The helicopter sound faded, the ships and children blinked back into view, and a snowball fight developed. Intrusions by *lessi*—and the danger they brought—were normal to clan children, but for Drago they were a long-endured infestation that he would soon eliminate.

This man's instinctive move to protect a child, and then his desire to protect all of his clan's children, says something about his values. Only later will the reader learn how his way of achieving his goals has been distorted by a murderous desire for vengeance. And it took very little narrative space to add this grace note to his character.

Storytelling
Create a really good bad guy

I'm bringing Vladimir back to illustrate creating a "good" antagonist. By that I mean a strong, interesting, and maybe even likeable character. Through the insights of an editor who critiqued one of my novels, I became aware of the need, and realized how to do it. Here's what we know of good old Vlad:

> Vladimir's blade sliced open Johnson's throat. The child-killer toppled, hands clutching his neck. Vladimir watched him writhe, and then become still. The bittersweet taste of vengeance filled Vladimir, and he smiled.

He has killed, but for a good reason—maybe. At this point, Vladimir could be the protagonist or the antagonist, although a reader is likely to be rooting for anyone who kills a child-killer. In this initial ambiguity lies a key to creating a good bad guy. We'll return to Vladimir later to resolve the ambiguity with more of the narrative.

My first novel, as initially written, wasn't all that good. But it contains themes I care about, and the core of a good story. Being a persistent fellow, I've rewritten it at least a half-dozen times. An agent represented it for a time, but it never sold. So I determined that, by damn, I'd publish it myself. I'm working on that as I write this book.

Faced with the prospect of strangers looking at my book with a critical eye, and asking them to spend money for it, I wanted to make sure that it was as good as it could be. I needed fresh eyes. Highly professional fresh eyes. So I, an editor, hired an editor, Lou Aronica, the aforementioned editor and publisher of bestsellers for a couple of top publishing imprints.

His critique exposed shortcomings in both character and plot, and he gave me guidance for lifting the novel to a truly publishable level. One problem was a primary antagonist. Lou said he wasn't strong enough or smart enough to be an interesting character, and I finally understood that he was right.

I wrote this book five novels ago as of this writing, and I'll admit that the bad guys were created just to be bad, just to attack the good guys. I didn't like the bad guys, and I didn't want my readers to like them either. So all of their characteristics are unlikeable—they are weak, corrupt, greedy, cowardly, dishonest, arrogant, and not all that bright.

Cartoony, to be honest, but I couldn't see that then. So there I was, faced with what to do with this cartoonishly nasty, inept, cowardly guy.

How do you make a guy you really don't like appealing?

An "aha" experience arrives

Finally it hit me. I needed to treat the antagonist like a protagonist. After all, he's the protagonist in *his* story, right? He believes in what he does, and that he's doing the right thing. It doesn't matter that I disagree with him or that the things he will do are evil. What matters is that for him they are the right thing to do, and that his cause is just.

We're all like that, aren't we? Even when we do something we know is wrong, we do it anyway because, at that moment in our lives, it's the right thing to do. Think of that last piece of chocolate cake you knew you shouldn't eat. . .

Bad guys don't think of themselves as bad guys. They're the heroes. So a narrative that intimates this person is bad and what he's doing is nefarious isn't true to character. And it's character that makes a novel interesting and convincing.

Take Vladimir. He seems to have excellent motivation for brutally killing a man. He clearly believes that it's the right thing to do. Since the victim had killed a child, we may even be on his side, emotionally.

But what if it develops that his victim is a doctor who has performed legal abortions that Vladimir opposes? Or perhaps, less controversial, a surgeon whose child patient died in surgery though no fault of his own? And this is the fifth physician Vladimir has killed? So now good old Vlad is a serial killer, and a very sick puppy.

I'm sure I had read advice on thinking about an antagonist as the star of his own story, but I had never internalized it. Once this epiphany finally hit—and I imagine that for many of you this is old hat—I started thinking again about how to portray my good/bad guy. The way the narrative delivers what he thinks and does shouldn't signal that he or his actions are evil, because, to him, they're not. And if the reader starts out feeling some empathy for this guy and his goals, then the arc of his story will be bigger and more dramatic.

Also, the smarter and stronger my bad guy is, the stronger the conflict, and the stronger my protagonist will be when he finally wins. Greater conflict! Bigger stakes! More tension!

The point is, once I viewed the world from inside his (now smarter) head, even my word choices changed. The way he reacts to people and events in his world changed. From his viewpoint, I was able to see my good guy as a bad guy.

Holy schizophrenia!

I must confess that it's difficult to shift the narrative and exposition—the word choices—from painting a picture of a nasty guy to one of someone who isn't, as far as we can tell. But that kind of ambiguity helps create a character with depth. By the way, it's also a good tactic to create unlikeable aspects for your good guys to create richer characters.

Here is the how the new version of my antagonist is introduced.

Kurt Dengler aimed his grandfather's Colt .45 automatic at Noah Stone's photo and cocked the hammer.

Stone smiled up at the Colt's muzzle from a *Time* magazine cover; the headline read, "Pied Piper of the West."

Kurt squeezed the trigger, the firing pin clicked on the empty chamber, and there was no hole in the enemy's forehead.

Like Daddy used to say, if wishes were horses, beggars would ride.

Kurt used his cell phone to call the number only he, the First Lady, and the Secret Service had. The president's deep voice said, "Hey, Kurt."

"We need to talk about a problem that needs to go away, Mr. President."

Leo chuckled. "You're my chief of staff, why don't you see if you can work you in?"

Not in the Oval Office, not with all those microphones. "Remember when we were kids, talkin' about running away?"

"Got it. The garden. Now's good."

Kurt hung the .45 on its pegs at the bottom of his grand-father's plaque. Beneath a Bronze Star medal, a brass plate read, "Major Jefferson T. Dengler." His grandfather hadn't made it home from World War II, but his heroism and his sidearm had. Kurt used his tie to polish away a fingerprint, snatched up the *Time* and the new polls, and left his West Wing office for the Rose Garden.

Events, Kurt's passion for the kind of country he thinks is right, his love for the president, and, of course, weaknesses, cause this character to orchestrate events that lead to the assassination of a good man. But at this point, you don't know that, do you? With his clear respect and affection for his grandfather's memory, he's even likeable.

He's a good bad guy.

Storytelling
Haunt characters for stronger storytelling

When I was in Hollywood, working at breaking into screenwriting, I took courses. One was Robert McKee's excellent workshop. Another was from a different screenwriting guru, John Truby. McKee's was all about structure (as is his highly recommended book, *Story*). But Truby got into other aspects of storytelling, including characterization.

An idea from his course that has stuck with me and proved useful is his notion that characters should have a "ghost." We're not talking about a haunt from Casper the Friendly Ghost, but a powerful, transformative event in a character's past that, whether consciously or not, affects his current behavior.

A now-clichéd example is childhood abuse suffered by a serial killer. It's a true-to-life ghost, but nowadays is becoming ho-hum. Authors now work to make their character's abuse more unique and horrific than competing killers, but it remains a standard serial-killer ingredient. And it is used to motivate the behavior of other troubled characters, and rightfully so—abuse is a powerful "ghost."

A violent ghost such as abuse is a good motivator for an antagonist, but I look for other things to trouble my characters. I'm most concerned with finding ghosts for my protagonists. I seek to write about flawed characters, and for me a ghost is one of the best ways to create a weak spot in a character.

My character ghosts are usually deep-seated and not necessarily conscious. The primary requirement is that it—the past event—still influences behavior. I don't necessarily make my readers aware of the ghost, certainly not early on. But, to have credible motivation, aspects of the haunt need to be revealed along the way. If conquering the ghost is part of the character's final epiphany, then it will be revealed.

Here's a tragic ghost for one of my primary protagonists. Jake shot and killed his wife in an unsuccessful attempt to save the life of his five-year-old daughter who his wife, in the grip of psychosis, kills. He deeply loved her, and the event was so traumatic that he has no conscious memory of it. He knows the facts—they were all in the police report—but he cannot recall what happened. It is, however, the content of a recurring nightmare.

More than that, this ghost has caused a kind of fugue in Jake—his emotions have shut down entirely to prevent further emotional injury. If you don't love someone, they can't hurt you.

This ghost in Jake's past affects everything in his day-to-day life: his relationships with other people, especially women; how he reacts to small children; and how he lives his professional life. He is an ex Secret Service agent turned mercenary, able to kill without conscious remorse or hesitation. Note that I said "conscious"; his ghost affects even his reaction to killing, and leaves him feeling nauseated after he kills.

Jake has an unconscious desire to break the thrall of his fugue and to conquer his ghost. When cracks begin to appear as a result of what happens to him in the course of the novel, he is eventually drawn to widening them and, finally, taking a gigantically risky route to conquering his ghost. When it is at last exorcised, his behavior changes, and that affects the climax of the story.

In a different novel, a coming-of-age story, the sixteen-year-old hero is haunted by the death of his father. It is more conscious in this story, but still an event that affects his thinking and motivates behavior, especially during the climactic conflict.

I urge you to find a ghost for your most important "unhaunted" characters, even if you're already into your project. You may be surprised at how it can change your character's reactions to the events and barriers you throw into her path along the way.

**WHAT ARE
THOSE LITTLE
WEIRD THINGS
IN TAPIOCA
PUDDING**

Storytelling

It takes story questions to turn pages

To keep a reader reading—*especially* an agent or editor overwhelmed with submissions—I believe a narrative must continually spark story questions in a reader's mind. Emphasis on *continually:* please, no scenic side trips. There's no more important time to sprout questions than when your novel opens. I learn best by example, so I thought a look at how some of the pros do it might be helpful to you. These are from books on my shelves.

Anne Rice opens *The Witching Hour* with this:

> The doctor woke up afraid. He had been dreaming of the old house in New Orleans again. He had seen the woman in the rocker. He'd seen the man with the brown eyes.
>
> And even now in this quiet hotel room above New York City he felt the old alarming disorientation. He'd been talking again with the brown-haired man. Yes, help her. *No, this is just a dream. I want to get out of it.*

Even the first sentence raises a story question: Why is the doctor afraid?

I was enthralled by Alice Sebold's *The Lovely Bones*. Here's how it drew me in with a story question provoked by the second sentence.

> My name was Salmon, like the fish; first name, Susie. I was fourteen when I was murdered on December 6, 1973. In newspaper photos of missing girls from the seventies, most

looked like me: white girls with mousy brown hair. This was before kids of all races and genders started appearing on milk cartons or in the daily mail. It was still back when people believed things like that didn't happen.

If that voice alone isn't enough to hook you, don't you just have to keep reading long enough to find out what happened to Susie? And note that the author slips in an "active" description of the character in the context of the story question and the character's thoughts.

I like openings that involve you with the protagonist right away. Here's the opening from *The Footprints of God*, by Greg Iles. The first paragraph raises a question that forces you to read further.

> "My name is David Tennant, M.D. I'm professor of ethics at the University of Virginia Medical School, and if you're watching this tape, I'm dead."
>
> I took a breath and gathered myself. I didn't want to rant. I'd mounted my Sony camcorder on a tripod and rotated the LCD screen in order to see myself as I spoke. I'd lost weight over the past weeks. My eyes were red with fatigue, the orbits shiny and dark. I looked more like a hunted criminal than a grieving friend.

Story questions don't, however, have to be limited to what's happening plot-wise; they can be about the character. Here's how Pulitzer Prize winner Carol Shields opens *Unless*:

> It happens that I am going through a period of great unhappiness and loss just now. All my life I've heard people speak of finding themselves in acute pain, bankrupt in spirit and body, but I've never understood what they meant. To lose. To have lost. I believed these visitations of darkness lasted only a few minutes or hours and that these saddened people, in between bouts, were occupied, as we all were, with the useful monotony of happiness. But happiness is not what I thought. Happiness is the lucky pane of glass you carry in your head. It takes all your cunning just to hang on to it, and once it's smashed you have to move into a different sort of life.

We've all suffered loss and unhappiness, and the questions in my mind include wondering what caused hers and how she would deal with it.

Harlen Coben begins *No Second Chance* with this:

> When the first bullet hit my chest, I thought of my daughter.
>
> At least, that is what I want to believe. I lost consciousness pretty fast. And, if you want to get technical about it, I don't even remember being shot. I know that I lost a lot of blood. I know that a second bullet skimmed the top of my head, though I was probably already out by then. I know that my heart stopped. But I still like to think that as I lay dying, I thought of Tara.

The opening of one of my manuscripts.

> Just after dark, death grabbed me by the tail. The moon was out, cool September breezes were scented with hints that fall was coming, and I was trotting over a mound of fresh earth, not an uncommon thing in a graveyard. My mind was on a svelte little Siamese over on 15th Street who was coming into heat when a hand shot up out of the dirt and clamped onto my rear extremity.

Are you ready to put the book down? *(I hope not. How embarrassing.)*

So how does the opening of your novel compare to the examples above? It doesn't have to be similar in technique—these vary widely—but it does have to raise questions that are going to make your mind itch for a good scratch that only your story can give.

Once you've got your novel launched, the narrative has to do two things:

1. Answer some of the questions you raise
2. Bring up new ones—like a bird following a trail of seeds, the reader sees the next seed just as he eats one…and so the story moves and pages turn

During the course of the middle, smaller questions are continually raised and answered. But you don't want your reader to reach the end of a chapter feeling that this would be a good place to put your book down. There should *never* be a good place to put your book down.

Storytelling

Chapter endings

A writer asked me this:

> How about chapter endings? Must they always end with a
> cliff hanging, hyperventilating, page turning, stomach churn-
> ing, my-God-I-ripped-the-pages-trying-to-find-what-comes-
> next? I just realized my ms is structured chronologically and
> some chapters seem to end naturally with everyone going to
> sleep at the end of a day, and I'm looking for excuses to
> leave it as it is.

I know what you're facing. The story is moving along. A chapter seems
solid, it advances the plot, or characterizes, or both. It feels good. But your
mental knuckles aren't clenched at the end. Is that a problem? Could be, unless you have underlying tension from before that's building.

Agent Cherry Weiner once took a look at a period mystery of mine. Her
rejection letter told me that "the characters were good and the story was interesting. But I could put it down."

From all I've read and heard, that's what both agents and acquisitions
editors are looking for—something they don't want to put down. How hard
is that to do, if the story is interesting and the characters good?

I know I haven't answered the original question yet, but context is important. An agent has requested a manuscript based on a query letter, so it's
sorta screened (a great query letter does not always lead directly to a great

read). She's received hundreds of submissions, many of which are interesting or have good characters. The brain cells the woman uses to evaluate fiction have calluses. What do you think it's going to take to create a story she doesn't want to stop reading?

And she knows something you don't—the fiction market is so tight and so tough that many acquisitions editors are turning more and more to non-fiction just to find something they feel they can recommend for publication. Your novel has to be something that keeps these equally jaded readers from setting the manuscript aside.

Keep in mind that this book is about *compelling* storytelling. I think that to succeed with fiction in today's market, every chapter must compel the reader to turn the page because they gotta know what happens.

Does this necessarily mean that every chapter must "always end with a cliff hanging, hyperventilating, page turning, stomach churning, my-God-I-ripped-the-pages-trying-to-find-what-comes-next?"

What every story must do, whether at chapter beginning, middle, or end, is raise story questions that are so provocative, so engaging, so rife with intrigue, that the reader is compelled to keep reading. When I reread the novel that Cherry Weiner rejected, I came to places where I felt I could put it down. She was right. I sent it to my then agent and, even though he loved the two novels he was representing at the time, he couldn't seem to finish reading that one. I haven't spent the time to figure out how to fix it yet, but that's the tough truth.

But story questions can be cumulative; they can add up to create an overriding level of tension in the reader. It's that level of tension that carries readers through exposition and description. And I think it can affect the reader's take on a fairly benign chapter.

Midway into one of my novels, a protagonist has just escaped torture and death at the hands of a not-so-ethical Homeland Security agent. The reader knows that he will continue to be pursued. He can't return to his life. He's lost his job. He's on the run. And the reader knows much more about the character that makes her want him to be okay.

The reader also knows that the man who helped our hero escape has a nefarious use for him that will lead to the deaths of many people. In this context, the protagonist reaches what seems like a safe haven with his rescuer. He is cared for and, even more fun, is seduced by a beautiful, provocative young woman. The chapter ends in the midst of their love-making.

So the chapter doesn't literally end with a cliff-hanger, but the story questions in the reader's mind are so powerful by then that putting those questions on hold for a moment of peace actually *increases* the tension in the reader because she knows trouble is coming, bigtime. Another example of continuous microtension.

And therein lies the best answer I have for the question. It may be fine for a chapter to end without people dangling over the edge of a precipice *if* the reader knows that terrible trouble is inevitable and coming on strong. In that case, surely the tension is increased. But I think this technique must be used with care.

The non-cliffhanger chapter must still be riveting in its own way, with unanticipated twists and turns that keep story questions coming. And I don't think you can defer getting back to the white-knuckle part for too long, else the reader will put your book down.

In some texts on screenwriting it's suggested that if act one ends on a negative note for the protagonist, then act two should end positively. It is the contrast that helps create tension. Stories must have rising tension, but along the way there should be brief respites. Without valleys, there are no peaks.

However, all that said, I'm going to work darned hard to make sure that every chapter I write (and edit) does end with a clear sense of compelling tension.

I think you owe it to all the work you've done on your novel to step back, take a look, and use your talent as a storyteller to make sure the tension crackles throughout the narrative. I'll bet you can end those going-to-sleep chapters with tension quivering. If it's difficult for you to see where the narrative needs injections of pressure, find informed, story-smart fresh eyes to help you see. We all need fresh eyes to make judgments about tension and story questions because we just can't totally trust our own. We know too much, and we love our stories too much, to see the saggy places.

> "I think writers assume that good writing is enough. Well, it's not."
>
> Kristin Nelson, literary agent

Storytelling

You have to go beyond strong writing

Story is the thing, but not just any old story told in an ordinary way. You need something that somehow takes you to a place you never thought about going. The phrase "fresh and original" is hackneyed, but those are the criteria a new author needs to break in.

Here's what Kristin Nelson, literary agent, said in her blog.

> I've been reading a lot of fulls lately and it occurred to me that there are a lot of strong writers out there—writers with enough talent to break into publishing but the current manuscripts I'm reviewing probably won't be the ones to open the door.
>
> I think writers assume that good writing is enough. Well, it's not. You have to couple good writing with an original storyline—something that will stand out as fresh and original. A story never told in this way before (even if elements are similar to what is already out on the market).

Case in point: when I was in Hollywood working on screenwriting, I got good at writing screenplays. Agents and others gave me feedback that let me know I had mastered the form.

I acquired an agent, and my scripts had all the elements: good dialogue; good action; good tension; good descriptions.

I was frustrated when nothing sold, but then I realized what I *didn't* have: a story strong enough to make someone invest a couple of years and millions of dollars into making a movie about it.

I was story impaired. This is not to say that they weren't good, interesting stories. They were. But they didn't take you to places you'd never dreamed of in particularly dramatic or special ways.

The television series we watch can get away with stories that reek of familiarity because they're free to us. You don't have to invest much in a TV series story. But a book—you pay hard cash, and then spend all that time reading.

> "There's a lot of good writing, but that doesn't necessarily add up to a good book."
>
> Chuck Adams, Executive Editor
> Algonquin Books

The agent you're hoping to hook up with wants a story that will not let her put the book down. I told you about the agent who rejected my manuscript because she could put it down. That was a story problem, not a writing problem.

Harsh reality. When you submit a partial or full manuscript to an agent, you're asking her to invest her most valuable resource—her time. Think of a story as having cash value. You need to buy her time, and you'd better be ready to ante up some serious story value.

The same goes with acquiring editors at publishing houses. Your submission is asking them to spend:

➢ Time—of which they don't have enough.
➢ Credibility—they have to sell your book to a committee, and then to the sales guys.
➢ Money—they've got to ask the company to spend thousands on getting your book to market.

All these people know that their target audiences want one thing—story.

Be tough on yourself and ask the hard question: Is my story unique enough. . .strong enough. . .fresh enough. . .?

I look at my novels and, to be honest, don't think some will rise far enough above the sea of submissions to snare a contract.

But then there's one that revolves around my unique take on the vampire legend. Since it concerns vampires, let's tune in to Kristin again.

Recently, I had the pleasure of reading three full paranormal novels featuring Vampires. All three were really well written. Had interesting characters that were developed. And even had interesting twists to the Vampire plot to make it unique.

Sounds good, right? So what happened?

The scenes the writers chose to create (in order to unveil the plot) were almost identical in each novel. I literally could have taken scenes out of one novel and plopped them into another and it wouldn't have impacted the story much.

I wasn't worried about my story until she listed some of the repetitive elements in the three novels. Her list starts with:

1. The backstory of how the vampire was made in the first place.

Dang. My novel starts with my hero being turned into a vampire. On the other hand, at least it's not backstory, it's the inciting incident.

Heh-heh, but the fresh thing is that the hero/narrator is a kitty-cat. Will that meet Kristin's criteria of "A story never told in this way before (even if elements are similar to what is already out on the market)"?

A couple more from her list:

2. Opening scene where the two main protagonists (usually male and female) are enemies but somehow must break through the barrier to work together. This usually involves a violent, confrontational scene to jumpstart the narrative. This scene usually happens in a dark place.

3. The main protagonists are being chased or must travel in order to accomplish what must be done. This is usually done in a car and there are motel/hotel scenes.

Sounds pretty mundane when she abstracts scenes like that, doesn't it? My story doesn't exactly follow that pattern—except for the violence and the darkness (hey, they're vampires), and the car (but it's a hearse!)—so I feel I can hope that this will escape the curse of "oh, that again."

But I'm sure going to think about it. Can I make those scenes more unique? Hmmmm. . .

This reminds me of a lesson from somewhere along the line that had to do with screenwriting, but it applies equally well to a novel. Let's say you want to write a scene in which two people tell each other they love one another.

Imagine that scene set in a lovely restaurant, with great service by the waiter, music in the background, etc.

Pardon the yawn.

Now imagine the same scene at the side of a freeway while the pair scrambles to change a flat tire as cars race past. Maybe even a drive-by shot rings out. Don't you think the emotions, the dialogue, the action will be much more riveting?

Section 2: Description

Without description, a novel would be no different than a printout of a radio commercial. We're all familiar with the primary purpose of description:

To show a place or illustrate action

But when you write for effect, description doesn't stop there. As you'll see, description is capable of this:

Adding to characterization

That's the plus side. There are hazards to avoid in description, too:
- Conclusion words
- Goofy staging of action
- Overwriting

First up: experiential description, a key tool for characterization.

"The light just came on. This is the best piece of advice on writing I've read in a long time."

J.D. Fox, writer

Description
Make it *experiential* to characterize

The reader of a novel wants the narrative to create a very specific effect: he wants to be taken away from the real world he sits in. He wants to feel and see and do things he would never do. Readers want to *experience* the world of the novel.

That's your task: to create an experience. It is not to *tell* a story. It is to cause a specific reaction in your reader's mind. A suspension of disbelief, a connection to the life of a character. Characters are the key to and core of creating an experience for the reader.

This relates to the old saw, "show, don't tell." *Telling* is the mere delivery of information. A newspaper does that. A novel should be delivering a character's experience. (Note: I'll italicize *telling* and *showing* whenever I'm referring to that craft aspect of creating a narrative.)

Description is a key element of every novel, every scene. Scenes need to be set (described) so the reader has a context within which to experience what the character experiences. It's needed to show action, of course. In a novel, descriptions shouldn't be simple photographs of what the character sees. Oh, they can be and often are, but snapshots don't create an experience. They are *telling*, they are information, they are not emotion, they are not experience.

The best description happens from within the character's point of view, colored by the character's emotions, needs, beliefs, and desires.

It characterizes.

Describe from the inside, not the outside

Here's description from a writer's sample where characterization could have happened but didn't. The writer describes Jimmy and his girlfriend this way:

> Jimmy was high-school skinny, that lean, still-growing time when muscles are tight everywhere and the sinews are loose and respond quickly. He wasn't tall, only five seven, but she was only five three and they appeared to be the perfect couple.

I liked "high-school skinny," but these lines are clearly the author getting some exposition out of the way—we're taken out of the boy's head and made to feel distant from the scene. The phrase "they appeared to be the perfect couple" is clearly from another point of view entirely, since the boy can't see what they look like together. Not to mention a first-degree case of *telling*.

I know it's tough to describe a character when you're in his point of view, and you don't want to resort to the tired old idea of looking in a mirror, but there are ways to do it. For example:

> Jimmy worried Kathy would think he was too skinny, which his mother said was just because he was still growing, all sinewy with long lean muscles. But he wasn't so worried about being only five foot seven—Kathy was maybe five three, tops, and he thought they made a perfect couple.

As you can see, this gives a picture of them but characterizes him as well, and it comes from inside the character, not from outside, from the author. The reader not only doesn't leave the character's head, she is drawn more deeply into it.

Experiential description of place

When you "see" a place through a character's point of view, you can do two things at once: set the scene to give the reader the context in which things are happening, and show a character's personality.

Here's an example: a mailroom in a large corporation seen as a simple snapshot, the approach many writers take to description.

In a gray room with fluorescent lights, a rack of pigeonholes for sorting mail sat along one wall. Next to them stood a wheeled delivery cart, a desk with a computer on it, and a worn swivel chair.

Now let's describe that same setting in a way that characterizes a middle-aged man who works in the mailroom.

Jeff switched on the mailroom lights. The fluorescents glared at him the way they had for fifteen years, and the gray walls radiated depression. The rack of pigeonholes for sorting mail along one wall stared at him, each empty hole like his life. The delivery cart stood ready to cause the daily pain in his hip when he trudged through the offices, delivering mail to people who didn't see him, like he was furniture.

On his desk the computer waited to be turned on—no, they said "booted up," didn't they—its programs lurking, waiting to trip him up again when he tried to send out a shipment. He sat in his beat-up swivel chair, and a small sense of comfort came with the way the worn cushions conformed to his body and it squeaked when he tilted back.

Just as the snapshot approach did, this experiential description gave you a picture of the room and what was in it, so it served the purpose of setting the scene. But it also defined Jeff's character.

The same room seen through another character's point of view has the same physical characteristics, but can be a very different place. Here's the room described through the point of view of Jinny, a twenty-something new employee.

Jinny burst through the mailroom door and was disappointed yet again to see Jeff already there. One of these days she'd beat him in and do the setup. He hadn't even turned on the computer yet. She reached past him, slumped as usual in that crummy old swivel chair with the ratty cushion—why didn't he requisition something decent?—and flicked on the computer. When break came and he went out for a smoke she'd surf her favorite blogs.

The gray walls under the soft fluorescent light soothed her headache. The racks of pigeonholes waited for her to fill their mouths with the mail that helped the company function. The delivery cart stood ready—maybe today she'd ask Jeff if she could be the one that wheeled it through the cubicles, saying hi, meeting people. Even though she'd only been here a month, the mailroom felt like an old friend.

"Wow, it is amazing how each example is quite clearly a different place, yet actually the same!"

M.S. Jackson, writer

Same pigeonholes, same everything picture-wise, but very different characterization—that's experiential description.

Whenever we step into a room, we not only see what's in it, we react to it in ways that characterize us. Have your characters do the same, and color their perceptions with the result.

Experiential description of action

Experiential description means that the exact same action, as experienced by two different characters, is a very different experience for each character and, thus, for the reader. First, the objective camera technique.

Morticia leaned forward and her nostrils flared. She sank her fangs into Frank's neck. Blood rushed into her mouth and dribbled down his neck. He moaned and writhed, but she pinned him to the wall and continued to drink his essence.

The thing is, characters aren't cameras. They're experiencing this action, not watching it happen. And their experience flavors the action with meaning. So here's this action from Morticia's point of view.

Morticia leaned forward. The scent of Frank's blood, pulsing just below the skin of his neck, aroused her. Her fangs lengthened and she sank them into a vein. The sweetness of blood washed over her tongue and poured down her throat. His moan aroused her further, and when he writhed within her grip, power rushed through her and she pinned him to the wall, drinking in the smell of his fear and relishing the rich taste of his essence.

Do you think Frank's experience of the very same action will feel the same as Morticia's? Hardly.

Frank shrank back when Morticia leaned forward, panic pounding in his mind. She was…smelling him? Oh, God, she had fangs, and they grew as he watched. She struck and twin points of pain pierced his neck. Hot liquid trickled down his neck—his blood? A moan crawked out of his throat and he writhed, pushing with all his strength to escape. As if he were a child, she jammed him against the wall with terrible power.

Now, I'm not claiming that the above examples are great writing—hey, I just pulled them out of the air. But I do think that the technique illustrated is valid—no, vital—to creating an experience for your reader. Describe, yes, but flavor the scene with how the character feels it, experiences it. Even a color can have meaning. Which of these gives you experience versus information?

Sheila's dress was blue.

Sheila's dress was the same sleazy blue Steve's mother had worn whenever she went out to get drunk.

I came across an elegant use of this technique in *The Silver Swan,* by Benjamin Black. A woman watches a man who could simply be described as lean and lanky, but the author helps us perceive him through her eyes in a way that characterizes both of them.

What a lovely loose way he had of walking, leaning down a little way to one side and then the other at each long, loping stride he took, his shoulders dipping in rhythm with his steps and his head sliding backwards and forwards gently on its tall stalk of neck, like the head of some marvelous, exotic wading bird.

Enough shown?

On the other hand

There are no rules. I feel obliged to point out that, while I think fiction that utilizes experiential description in key passages is stronger and more engaging, it isn't the only way to deliver a fascinating story.

The reason I feel obligated to point this out is that as I was polishing this manuscript, I picked up Stephen King's *The Eyes of the Dragon*. Published in 1988, it's King doing his thing with the classic fairy tale—the good prince and the bad prince, the evil magician, dragons. . .

And Stephen tells the tale. His voice is the storyteller's voice, and once in a while he speaks directly to you. He's not rendering the experience of the characters, and I'm distant from the story, much more of an observer than a participant.

Because of King's voice, and the fun of the tale, I'm having a great time. The distance from the story doesn't matter, it's fun because I have a gifted storyteller's voice whispering in my ear.

Just sayin'.

However, that is not to say that the same story, and the same characters, couldn't have been more powerful illustrations of how to be a person if they'd been written in a different way. That's the beauty of being a writer— you have an amazing amount of control over exactly what the reading experience will be: the reader's emotional involvement, her intellectual involvement, her takeaway.

It's your bus to drive, your road to take, just make the trip as good as you can.

Inhabit characters to deliver *their* experience

When an author story-tells well, a reader comes to inhabit a character, seeing and feeling as the character does—identifying with him. This is a good thing because if a reader cares about what happens to a character, she is compelled to read more (as long as interesting things happen, of course).

I'm a "pantser"—a writer who creates by the seat of his pants with no outline, as opposed to "architects" who plan ahead with an outline. I'm not one for creating character profiles that list everything from religion to shoe size. For me to generate narrative that draws a reader into a character, I shoehorn myself into a character's head to play the scene from there, to truly "see" so actions and reactions correspond to *that* reality. I recently applied this technique to introduce a new character and setting.

Going into that scene, all I knew was plot material: the character's name and his role as an antagonist. I knew that he was inside a vehicle in which he traveled and lived. I knew the outside of the vehicle was wooden, and that he was in a forest preserve outside of Chicago in wintertime. I didn't even know what kind of vehicle he was in. That was about it.

When I inserted myself into my character's head and looked around, the first thing I discovered was that the room he was in was paneled with oak, and that Oriental rugs covered the floor. Why? Because that's the way this character would want his living space—rich and opulent. As I looked more closely, I saw that the oak paneling bore carved scenes from the history of his people. And that led me to how to discover and describe the setting and character in ways that helped the reader feel something.

You've seen part of the following scene before in the discussion of caring about characters. Look at it this time for the environment he's in—it's the result of stepping inside that character's head and letting my subconscious deliver the details of his experience.

> The percussive *whup-whup-whup* of a helicopter drew Drago to a porthole in his galleon's quarterdeck cabin. In the forest clearing where his ship and two others of his clan rested, a half-dozen clan children, teens to toddlers, built a snowman. The tall curved hulls of the sixteenth-century Spanish vessels, all grace when they sailed through the air, now seemed awkward, supports angling out like spider legs to hold them upright. The daylight was dim under the gray January sky, but that didn't seem to matter to the children.
>
> The helicopter grew closer and smothered their giggles. The galleons vanished behind *glaméres* of snow-clad forest, the illusions broadcast by alert sentries.
>
> All save one of the children disappeared as well, disguised as young trees. Little Alexandra, her skills not yet awakened, burst into tears. Drago swung the porthole open to help her with a concealing *glamére*, but then a sapling scooped up the child. In the flicker of a thought, a fat squirrel appeared in her place. Satisfied, he closed the port against the chill.
>
> The helicopter sound faded, the ships and children blinked back into view, and a snowball fight developed. Intrusions by *lessi*—and the danger they brought—were normal to clan children, but for Drago they were a long-endured infestation that he would soon eliminate.
>
> He'd rather be basking in Louisiana sunshine with the rest of his clan, not skulking in a forest preserve on the outskirts of Chicago. But his research into recombinant DNA demanded top university libraries close to a good hiding place, and it had been worth it. He was near to ending the murder and destruction ordinary humankind visited upon the world, to a final solution for the *lessi* blight. He felt it. Perhaps *that* day, yes!

And then he would be revenged for the death of Graeme, his son gone forever, cut down in the prime of manhood by a *lessi*.

Drago shivered and gathered enough *lledri,* the living energy radiated by all things alive, to create a blanket of energy that hugged his skin and repelled the cold. Warm light from kerosene lamps gave the impression of comfort, but the cabin was unpleasantly chilly despite oaken wall panels and woolen Oriental rugs insulating the hardwood floor. The pot-bellied woodstove in the corner tempted him, but a column of smoke couldn't be hidden, and the danger of discovery was too great that close to a *lessi* city acrawl with people like maggots in a carcass.

He tested the cold coming off a wall panel with a fingertip, and then lingered to trace the carving there, a scene of his ancestor Merlin deep in conversation with King Arthur. The artist had portrayed Merlin as tall and lean, with a handsome beard that reached his chest. Drago wished he looked like the carving instead of the balding, plump appearance he associated with a ruddy-cheeked butcher in a small-town grocery store. He suspected that the real Merlin looked much like he did, and the majesty portrayed on the panel was no more than imagination at work.

None of this detail existed before I started to write the scene from *within* the character's head. This character became very human to me, with strong desires and a wistful wish that he still had his hair. (I hadn't really understood that he was bald.) This is another example of experiential description that characterizes as well as depicts.

I believe that, from this point on, the reader will want to know more about what happens to Drago even though he comes to do nasty things. A tough task, but I think it's possible if I can get the reader to inhabit Drago and view the world as he does.

In contrast, when reading *The DaVinci Code* I never felt a thing for any of the characters. I recall a lot of telling rather than dramatization, and they never became less than distant to me. For me, his characters were wooden pawns in a plot, not movers and shakers of their own lives. I never inhabited them, and I never cared. But I loved the background ideas and information.

Inhabit your characters so I can too.

With bright blue button eyes
and a tuft of red hair, Baby
Harry was adored from the
second he arrived.

Description

Use specifics to deliver what you intend

I enjoyed immensely *The Modern Library Writer's Workshop* by Stephen Koch, a noted teacher and author. One of the reasons is that he talks about storytelling in ways that resonate with the way I approach it.

One point he made that sparked for me is that we (the authors) haven't actually told our stories until someone reads them. Koch writes:

> To be sure, the reader follows the writer's lead; but only the reader's imagination, collaborating with the writer's, can make anything happen on any page. It's the reader who visualizes the characters, the reader who feels and finds the forward movement of the story, the reader who catches and is caught in the swirls of suspense, rides the flow of meaning, and unfolds the whole kaleidoscope of perception.

Our readers can do that—must do that—to experience our stories. Or, rather, their version of our stories. Each reader will add shades to the meanings of words and expressions and actions. They'll never read the story we've imagined.

Still, we hope a reader will experience our stories the way we feel them, and we can get 'em close, damn close, close enough, with strong craft. One aspect of craft, in particular, is the tool we need: specific, concrete details and imagery.

It's what author and teacher Oakley Hall in *How Fiction Works,* calls "specification," using concrete words and images rather than abstract words and generalizations. Here are wrong/right examples he gave.

1. He was a big man with a beard.
2. He filled the doorway, his beard glistening with curls.

1. It was cold in the kitchen.
2. She hunched her shoulders and rubbed her hands together against the chill in the kitchen.

1. The crowd passed in the street.
2. The street brimmed with the jostling of men in cloth caps and women in babushkas.

1. It was raining.
2. He drew his hand inside and licked raindrops from his fingertips.

Specificity makes your visualizations vivid and alive. And probably you "see" an image much closer to what the author imagined. Of Oakley's examples, the one about the cold kitchen does it best for me.

Without specific, concrete images, your reader might imagine something you never intended, and thus stray far from the story you wanted to tell. And it's important to make sure it's *your* story, not a walkabout made up of random associations to vague language.

Specificity has to do with writing for effect. Or maybe I should say writing *to affect*, to make sure the things that go on in your reader's mind are as close to your original thought as possible. Keep in mind the stimulus/response paradigm. What you put on the page—and *only* what you put on the page—kicks off neural responses in your reader that affect what she thinks, imagines, understands, and feels.

Description
Describing a point-of-view character

One of the first opportunities for a writer to break the spell he's weaving in the reader's mind is when the time comes to describe a character from within that character's point of view. You've seen the hackneyed "looks in a mirror" approach—although it works, it just isn't, well, *good*. But that's just one among many clumsy ways to add description. For example:

> She shook her long blond hair out of her eyes.

What's wrong with that? In my view, if you're close in a character's point of view, experiencing the story as they do, you don't include things the character would not think or do. If your hair is in your eyes, the thought in your mind isn't to get your long blond hair out of your eyes, it's simply to get your hair out of your eyes. In this example, adding "long blond" is an authorial intrusion that distances the reader from the character.

Maybe you don't even need to describe a character

Don't forget that you've got a reader out there, ready and eager to contribute to the vision. If you sketch in enough of a character's appearance for the reader to distinguish the character from others, the reader is perfectly capable of adding details to the picture in their mind. Being a participant in building the scene is part of the fun of reading.

When Elmore Leonard wrote in the *New York Times* about his ten rules of writing, he quoted a character from a John Steinbeck novel who says, "I don't like to have nobody tell me what the guy that's talking looks like. I want to figure out what he looks like from the way he talks."

Leonard goes on to say this:

> In Ernest Hemingway's *Hills like White Elephants*, what do the "American and the girl with him" look like?
> "She had taken off her hat and put it on the table."
> That's the only reference to a physical description in the story, and yet we see the couple and know them by their tones of voice, with not one adverb in sight.

Readers will indeed fill in the picture without much help from you. While the author may know what a character looks like, maybe the reader doesn't need to quite so much.

If there's something remarkable about a character's appearance that affects the story, then there's a clear need to describe. A couple of examples that come to mind:

➢ A character is so beautiful that she or he draws a crowd wherever she or he goes.

➢ A man who is so ugly that he can't find work because people can't look at him.

But if you do need to describe a character, there are several ways to do it.

The "character thinks about himself" approach:

In this example, we're in a teenager named Jesse's point of view. He's just remarked to his friend Dudley about a girl they've met who sparked a lot of interest in him.

> Dudley shrugged. "She was looking at you."
> Jesse could think of only one word for what she had seen—medium. Medium tall, medium brown hair, medium brown eyes, medium looks, medium build (if he could shed a couple pounds). Medium nobody.

Jesse's relatively low self-esteem gives the reader enough of a picture to go on. The passage continues, finding a way to give the reader Jesse's age, but doing it within the context of describing the girl, which leads to. . .

The "see a character through another's eyes" approach:

Jesse had figured the rancher's daughter for fifteen when they met at the ranch house that morning, so he had a year on her. But she was already the kind of girl a boy instantly undressed with his eyes.

It wasn't her body that had started his mental peep show, although she was fun to look at. She was small, five feet tip to toe, if that. His gaze had roamed happily down and back up slender, tanned legs exposed by short shorts, but on top she was no Playmate of the Month.

It was a boldness in her green eyes that promised the stuff of daydreams. And then her handshake had lingered, her fingertips trailing across his palm as they left.

I feel that this technique is *showing*, via Jesse's feelings and reactions about the girl, rather than *telling*. In this way the description of the girl characterizes both of them—it's much more than a simple snapshot, a list of features such as hair and eye color, height, weight, etc.

Here's how Jesse's friend Dudley was described, using the "another's eyes" approach. Here, past history between the friends helps characterize and describe at the same time:

Dudley moved in even slower motion. Big and powerful at six feet and on the fat side, every year the Wildcat football coach came after Dudley for the offensive line, and every year Dudley was too lazy for all that exercise. But his strength didn't seem to help today.

At this point in the narrative, the boss, the owner of the ranch the boys are working for, arrives on the scene.

Mister Braun fit Jesse's picture of a Texas rancher. Standing eye to eye with Jesse, he was lean, his tan skin like a tight leather glove. Gray peppering his long black sideburns made him look old to Jesse, maybe as old as forty.

The dust whitening his jeans looked like it belonged there, and the sweat darkening his shirt and straw cowboy hat looked like hard work. He wore heavy-duty shoes, not the boots Jesse had expected on a rancher.

You learn the boss's size—eye to eye with Jesse, who was "medium"—and have a picture of a middle-aged, lean man. But you also know something about his personality—he works hard enough to sweat a lot and doesn't mind getting dirty.

Descriptions can be lean (and I think should be, most of the time), but sometimes, if the character's appearance is a factor in the story because of how others react to her, I look for a way to build more of a picture. Here are two pieces that describe a character—Jewel, a woman in her twenties.

The "character reacts to others" approach:

> Murphy's piggy eyes stumbled across Jewel as she closed on him. His gaze went for its usual tour of her body—yeah, she was wearing a sleeveless, scoop-neck top and a mini-skirt, but what the hell, couldn't a girl enjoy a spring day without some slob feeling her up with his eyeballs?

Okay, now we know how she's dressed, and our imagination fills in a woman shapely enough to provoke such attention. The action continues with. . .

The "character reacts to events" approach:

> The breeze that swirled around the tall office buildings reeked of car exhaust, but her skin liked its touch even though the sky above was its usual beige. She basked in the sun's warmth, imagining she could feel it turning her gold-brown color a shade darker.

Now we know, sort of, the color of her skin. And something about her personality, a certain sensuality. But wait, there's more. . .

The "looks at a reflection" approach:

I think you can do this as long as it reflects a true point-of-view response.

> She stopped to eye a cupcake display in a restaurant window. In her reflection, her ice-blue eyes—donated by some honky ancestor—jumped out at her. So did the scar, a three-inch trail curving down her face from high on her cheekbone.

Jewel gave her body the once-over like Murphy had. Still lookin' good . . . wait a minute, was that a little bit of extra tummy? She turned sideways. Damn, gettin' poochy. She sucked in her gut and walked on, wrestling with whether to diet or exercise, or both.

This last descriptive part combines the "reflection" approach with the "thinks about self" technique in a believable and natural way. Her reflection is used to provoke thoughts that characterize (i.e. her concern about her figure) without the author telling the reader details about her figure.

Description

Color narrative to characterize

What a character says, thinks, and does is guided by personality, needs, perceptions, abilities and limitations. Of course. But I believe a writer should take that principle a level deeper: even expository narration should reflect the character's personality, should be *colored* by the character's persona in a way that creates a distinct voice in your reader's ear. That portion of the story should read as if the character has composed the narrative, *not* the author. Done well, once a reader is introduced to a character she will recognize a character's narrative even if the character is not named. Each character is a different color on your narrative pallet.

The key to doing this was brought home to me when a critique partner said, about a novel in progress that she was helping with, "I love the change of vocabulary accompanying the change in POV [point of view]." She referred to the word choices in the exposition part of the narrative, and had put her finger on the root technique for flavoring in a way that I hadn't thought of. It's the words, stupid.

How many popular novels fail to do this? I see them; don't you? While dialogue may differ (often not by much), exposition is flat and non-differentiated. But it could be different. I say it should be.

Here's an example of coloring a narrative from a suspense novel that takes place in the old West. When it shifts from one point of view to another, so does the voice of the narrative.

Wood thunked on wood and Zach whirled, his finger
tightening against the trigger. In the doorway to the sparc

room stood a boy of about ten. A boy propped on a crutch, his left leg hanging limp. A boy with Tom's long, serious face, his sandy hair, and his hazel eyes, eyes that fastened on Zach's. They widened. "Father?"

Zach turned to the woman. "Where's Tom Duval?"

She swayed and braced herself with a hand on the window sill. She stared at him.

He had to have an answer. "Who are you?"

She lifted her chin and leveled golden eyes at him. "His widow."

* * *

Amber felt him lookin' at her. Like all men did.

Except for the fancy city suit, he was the spittin' image of Tom. Same stocky body, strong-looking, the hazel eyes with arching brows that made his gaze seem like it was coming after her.

Why in hell did he have to show up? A few more days and she'd have been out of this inferno.

Here are the narratives about two characters in a speculative thriller.

A tiresome clump of a half-dozen gang jerks swaggered toward Jake with cocky menace and semi-automatic pistols visible. They blocked most of the sidewalk, forcing people to step off the curb or sidle along a building front. Jake locked his gaze onto the eyes of the guy in the center and walked straight at him.

The kid kept his cool as they came together, but one stride from colliding he dropped his gaze and sidestepped. Jake cut through, never slowing.

He focused on what he knew of the Attorney General. He'd heard from his old contacts in Justice that she was honest and devoted to the law, and that she hated the under-the-table deal-making of politics. He had too, at one time.

* * *

Two punks, slouching against a gun shop window, smacked kisses at Jewel. A green stripe ran down the center of the blond's buzz-cut hair. A red do-rag decorated the smaller guy's shaved head—he cupped his balls and licked his lips. Ugh. She picked up her pace, her mini-skirt riding high.

They pushed off from the store and swung into step on each side of her. Green-Stripe edged close. "Hey, Brown Sugar."

"I'm not your sugar." Keeping her gaze straight ahead, she said, "There's a cop back there."

"Yeah." He laughed. "Murphy."

His sour stink hit her. Her skin goose-bumped. Wishing she wasn't wearing high heels, she broke into a run.

Color narrative with the same vocabulary and style as a character's dialogue and you'll increase your odds of delivering the character's experience directly to your reader. Each character's turn on the stage will resonate as a *person*, not just a puppet you've trotted out to roll the plot wheel.

Description
Avoid conclusion words

Author Barbara D'Amato finds consistent factors in the work of beginning writers that kill the promise. One she talked about in a post for *The Outfit*, a multi-author blog by Chicago crime writers, struck me because it's something I'm constantly pointing out in my edits. I just didn't have this fine label for them that she used: "conclusion" words.

Barbara says she finds "too many 'conclusion' words: beautiful, arrogant, ugly, magnificent, ghastly, stately, scary, and so forth."

Here are a few more:

> handsome
> attractive
> momentous
> embarrassing
> fabulous
> powerful
> hilarious
> stupid
> fascinating

When used as description, these conclusion words are *telling*, and offer no real clue as to what the reader should be seeing. For example, what images come to mind when you read this description?

Allyson was beautiful.

Any picture of Allyson has to be reader-generated, and may have nothing to do with what the author intends. Beauty, being in the eye of the beholder, is subjective. You may think an anorexically thin Allyson to be beautiful while I think she should see a doctor. Steve may think that a woman with a good extra fifty pounds of love handles is beautiful while Roger thinks she should call Weight Watchers. And so on.

The difference between *telling* and *showing* usually boils down to the physical senses.

If the author wants us to think Allyson is beautiful, she needs to give us pictures that illustrate beauty, not labels.

> Allyson moved with a ballerina's grace, and her slim figure made any clothing look good. Long hair the color of dark chocolate framed a face that made Johnny think of a princess in a fairy tale, and he wanted to be the one to kiss lips that smiled and pouted and invited, all at the same time.

That's not to say that you should avoid the word beautiful. It can be quite useful in characterizing. For example, here's a descriptive passage in which two teenage boys are going to work on a ranch for the summer and go to a small log cabin that's to be their summer quarters.

> Excitement grew in Jesse as they approached the cabin. A place all their own. No grown-ups.
>
> Inside, they stood in a main room just big enough for a double bunk bed, a four-drawer dresser, two chairs beside a small table, and a little space left over to walk around. A battered old radio sat on the table, and an easy-going breeze wafted through the screened door and out the single side window.
>
> A doorway into the bathroom revealed an old-fashioned tub with feet; a metal bar suspended from the ceiling encircled it with a shower curtain. Jesse stepped to the door and looked in. The toilet had a seat but no lid, the sink a medicine cabinet above it, but the mirror was cracked.
>
> Beautiful.

So "conclusion" words can be useful when you use them to describe just that: a conclusion. Jesse concludes that the cabin is beautiful even though, to his mom, I'm certain it would be far from it.

In looking through samples from writers for "beautiful," I find examples that make Barbara's "conclusion" label clear.

> It's a beautiful day, so we drive to Lyme Park.

Can't see the day, can you?

> He gestures at a strikingly beautiful black woman sitting opposite him.

No picture there. Oh, we know the impact of the woman's appearance on our point-of-view character, but not what causes it. If we received a picture of the black woman, we'd learn what "beautiful" means to our POV character, and thus gain insight into his character. But in this case we learn nothing.

Here's an example where the conclusion word is at least followed by the description:

> They've got two little boys who are utterly beautiful—all huge blue eyes, blond hair and cheeky grins.

Here are some especially common conclusion words:
elegant
shabby
bizarre
eerie
weird (a very common one)
strange (another very common one)
eclectic
large or small (also relative terms meaningless without a comparison)

I suggest you do a search for the conclusion words from this section and any others you can think of and see if you've used them as description words—and then substitute the description.

Description

Stagecraft: don't trip over your imaginings

Staging is how action unfolds or how a character interacts with the setting. It's a necessary part of description, and one in which writers are particularly prone to lapses. Because they see the action so clearly in their minds, it's easy to leave out vital clues that the reader needs. Or sometimes it's the opposite—a character is racing through a high-action scene and the writer fails to see the action clearly. A writer can be so focused on the outcome she wants that she unwittingly bends possibility until it breaks.

The logic problems that bad staging creates raise two issues that become especially damning if the reader is an agent or acquisitions editor:

1. You lose credibility with the reader.
2. You confuse the reader, which can mean that she has to break out of the story to figure out what's going on, or might just stop reading altogether.

But there's a way to get your staging right. Slip into a character's skin, look around, and go through his motions. If you act out the action in your mind (much different than simply writing a description of it), you can keep it real. And sometimes it's a good idea to get off your chair and physically go through the actions you're describing.

Following are examples adapted from edits I've done. First I'll give you the excerpt, and then the comment I gave in the edit.

An elderly man shuffled toward them. He wore a hospital johnnie that dangled open in the back.

Comment: If he's coming toward the point-of-view character, the POV guy can't see that it dangles open in the back—you need to either cut this or fix the staging so that it can be seen.

See if you find this one confusing.

Looking over at him, she could not remember if she had ever made love in the afternoon, in a room with the shades up. A time when it did not matter if the sun had set, or the blinds were drawn, or the door locked to ward off children. But now, watching the leaves come down, she could not remember such a time.

Comment: At this moment you have her looking over at him as he sleeps, not watching the leaves and then suddenly she's watching leaves. Suggest you have her turn her gaze back to the leaves before her concluding thought.

For the next excerpt, the character is blindfolded and in a place she has never been.

As the man who had been holding her walked away, she could hear his feet echoing down the hall.

Comment: You had written this as if she could know he went down a hall, but it has to be a question because she can't see. Thought-starter: When the man who had been holding her walked away, she could hear his footsteps echo—down a hall?

In the following example, the character has picked up a basket on his front porch that contains a baby and taken it inside. Then this happens…

Holding the basket in my lap, I pulled the blanket aside.

Comment: Is he sitting somewhere? The living room? Kitchen? You need to set the scene a little so the reader can picture the character in action. Another thought: a basket large enough to hold a baby would be pretty big to put in your lap. Suggest he either set it on the floor or on the kitchen table.

Next, brevity creates confusion.

The Chevy glided over the bumps in the rutted road. Darkness had fallen as he slowed on the unfamiliar road looking for her house.

Comment: There's something wacky about the sense of this staging of darkness coming and the slowing of the car. It means that darkness came in/during the time it took him to slow down. Either darkness falls far more quickly where he lives than it does on my part of the planet, or he took an awful long time to slow down. You need to adjust the "reality" of this darkening.

And finally. . .

Once safely inside her flat on the fourth floor, she went to open her bedroom window. She recoiled behind the curtain when she saw a long shadow on the pavement below recede into darkness. She recognized him.

Comment: She saw only a shadow and yet she recognized him? Doesn't seem possible, especially if she is four stories up and it is dark outside. Need to rethink what the staging is here if you want her to see the guy well enough to recognize.

Moral: inhabit characters so you don't trip over the scenery. Act out the action in your mind to reveal gaps and impossibilities.

Second moral: find sharp "other eyes" to help spot goofs you can't see.

Description

Watch out for the incredibles

The "incredibles" appear when you have a character do something either improbable or impossible. I see manuscripts peppered with little impossibilities and improbabilities, although I suspect that many readers would never notice them. At least consciously. If noticed, they can take a reader out of your story and damage your credibility. The suspension of disbelief may be destroyed. I suspect that they are noticed at some level, even if not consciously, and do their damage. Here are some from work I've edited:

> He clenched his teeth and said, "I could kill you."

> "You always wanted to fly, Erin," he said through gritted teeth.

Okay, now you try clenching or gritting your teeth and saying anything intelligible. Don't fudge, keep your teeth clamped together. You'll note that not only can you not talk very well, but a character would look darned silly doing it. I find it unrealistic to portray a character talking like this. Writers have argued with me that it's possible, and yes, it is. Sort of like what a ventriloquist does. But have you ever, really, said something through tightly clenched teeth? I haven't, and I don't think a character would. If you want clenched or gritted teeth, separate them from the dialogue.

> He clenched his teeth and then said, "I could kill you."

Here's a subtle impossibility.

I bent down, gingerly touching the small gray bone.

The sense of the sentence is that he touched the bone *as* he bent down, but that's not right because the bone is on the ground and he can't touch it until *after* he bends down. More accurately:

I bent down and gingerly touched the small gray bone.

Here's a tidy impossibility:

He snarled silently.

A snarl is a sound, so you can't snarl silently. Your mouth can curl as if snarling, though.

A perennial favorite is using "eyes" in a silly way.

We stood for a long moment, our eyes locked.

So these people put their faces so impossibly close together that their eyes locked together? The writer means "gazes."

Arlene shifted her eyes to the piles of vegetables.

Really, eyes are much more functional when they stay in your head, don't you think? Another time when "gaze" was called for.

Here's a different "eye" thing:

She wiggled to a sitting position, her eyes sleepy but bright, tugging at the neck of her footy-pajamas.

This sentence has this person tugging at the neck of her jammys with her eyes. Weird.

How people use their bodies often suffers from a case of the impossibles. In the following example, the writer could clearly see the action in her mind, she just failed to get it on paper phrased in a clear way.

I wrapped myself around him and we dropped to our knees.

This leads me to picture someone wrapping their arms and legs around someone else, right? And then they both drop to their knees? Naw.

> I watched Ellen and her friend drive back to Studio City in their BMW as I waited for someone to answer my call.

Unless this character is in a helicopter or hot air balloon, he/she can't watch someone drive to another city. The writer really meant "depart for" Studio City.

> The voices began, too low to be heard.

If the character knows the voices begin, then he hears them. The writer meant that the words couldn't be *understood* because the voices were so low.

> She stood in the doorway blocking out the light on each side.

This means that the person was wider than the doorway and had somehow wedged her body into it, which seems highly unlikely.

> (a man looks at a diapered baby) I saw instantly that the baby was wet.

Nope. You can feel whether or not a diaper is wet, but you can't really see it, especially nowadays with disposable diapers.

These illustrate the need for fresh eyes. Sharp, picky eyes. Eyes that do not leave heads but instead stay put and search for the incredibles.

"Initially overwhelmed about all I felt I needed to know, the examples that you provide help synthesize concepts in my sometimes tired brain."

Grace, a writer

Description

Overwriting: the attack of killer verbiage

Some writers new to the task of the novel put in every possible nuance and detail of a scene or action—and drown their pace and tension in a sludge of words. Invisible and deadly, overwriting can suffocate a narrative.

Overwriting is insidious, and can grow just a word or two at a time. Here are two examples from a client's work:

> He tasted her in his mouth. *(Where else would he taste her?)*

> Her heart clenched in her chest. *(Better there than in her purse, I guess.)*

What pains me are far worse examples in published novels. Take the following trudge from *The Experiment* by John Darnton.

The scene: a woman enters a darkened bedroom. In the bed sleeps a man who she assumes is her love interest. Spreading minutiae like a blanket of kudzu, Darnton writes…and writes…and writes…

> She thought that perhaps she should try to take a nap, too; the trip home had exhausted her. She walked around the bed, sat in a chair and unstrapped her shoes and took them off, placing them to one side. She stood up and unzipped her dress, letting it fall to the floor in a heap and bent down to pick it up and drape it over the back of the chair. She slipped

her thumbs into the waist of her panties and slid them down her legs, placing them over the dress. Then she unfastened her bra and placed it on top. From the bed, she heard his breathing shift as he moved to a different level of sleep.

She walked to the right side of the bed, lifted the sheet and slipped underneath, pulling it up to her chin. The cotton felt cool to her skin.

Does the word "turgid" come to mind? If not, see a therapist immediately. Trust me on this: the entire purpose of this passage was to get the woman into the bed. Her method of disrobing had absolutely no bearing on anything that had gone before or anything that happened afterward.

It didn't matter that she walked around the bed. Or sat in a chair. Or where she placed her discarded shoes. Or what she did with her dress or bra. Nor did her panty-removal process have any bearing—the person in the bed was asleep, and there was no sexual intent to the scene. And it didn't matter which side of the bed she got into, either. Don't get me started on other deficiencies in this dawdle.

When it comes to description, I'm with Stephen King, as expressed in his *On Writing*. To quote from his book,

> Look—here's a table covered with a red cloth. On it is a cage the size of a small fish aquarium. In the cage is a white rabbit with a pink nose and pink-rimmed eyes. In its front paws is a carrot upon which it is contentedly chewing. On its back, clearly marked in blue ink, is the numeral 8.

As King points out, the paragraph doesn't tell us what the cage is made of. Wire mesh? Steel rods? Glass? It doesn't tell us because it doesn't matter. Whatever the reader "sees" allows him to visualize the rabbit inside and the most important story part of the description, the number on its back.

King says that good description makes the reader a participant in the story. Exactly right. Crisp, tight description lets the reader fill in the details, especially if they don't matter to the storyline.

In the above example from Mr. Darnton's book, all that verbiage boils down to this:

> Exhausted by the trip home, she thought she should try a nap. She undressed, slipped underneath the sheet and pulled it up to her chin, the cotton cool on her skin.

Here's a technique that might have helped Mr. Darnton avoid his logorrhea—read your narrative aloud. If, at some point, you detach and drift, your voice a drone in the background while your mind searches for something interesting to think about, your narrative has been binge expositing, and you need to apply the cure—vigorous exercise of the delete key.

Section 3:

Just as a novel without description would be a radio script, a novel without dialogue would be a word-picture book. To state the obvious, dialogue characterizes, illustrates, and moves action. So we needn't get into that.

But many writers find it difficult to craft smooth, credible, crisp dialogue. Some of the hazards are:

> ➤ Dialogue tags gone wrong
> ➤ Naked dialogue
> ➤ Over-use of "with"
> ➤ Bassackwards delivery of the sound of a speech

Well, this section can help.

> "Even when it's a 'lesson' that one has already applied, sometimes the style, manner, or direction of your advice light a bulb in my pointy little head and lead to improvement."
>
> Bernita, writer

Dialogue

Tags: a game writers shouldn't play

Because each of us has a lifetime of experience with talking, writing dialogue in a novel seems like it should be easy, and maybe it is for some writers. But for others it's the weakest part of their narrative. Three common flaws I see in beginning work are:

> ➤ Botched use of dialogue tags
> ➤ Lack of effective action beats
> ➤ Explaining the dialogue instead of *showing* it happen

Here's a snippet of dialogue guaranteed to make you flinch:

"Please don't do that," he articulated.
"What?" she interrogated.

Okay, perhaps that's a touch over the top. But how many times have you seen dialogue tags like the following?

Melissa turned to Irving. "Why don't you zip up your pants?" she asked.
He shrugged. "Air conditioning," he replied.

What's with "she asked" and "he replied"? The question mark clearly tells the reader that a question was asked, and the response is clearly a reply, and the reader damn well knows what they were. Yet "she asked" and the ever-popular "he replied" clog thousands of pages like verbal cholesterol.

When it comes to dialogue tags, a couple of clichés should be applied:

1. Less is more.
2. KISS—Keep It Simple, Stupid

Tags can tangle dialogue and slow pace; their absence can smooth and accelerate. Over-explanatory tags (he huffed, she whimpered) create lazy writing; replacing them with action or description gives the words meaning and tone that involves the reader, creates pictures, and enhances emotional effect.

Rarely is there a need for a dialogue tag other than "said," even with a question. For example, there's no need to use "asked" or "interrogated" or "queried" if you write

Farnsworth said, "Where do you think the monster is hiding?"

The reader understands that Farnsworth has asked a question—that's what question marks are for. To add tonality, use description and action, and remove the "said." For example:

Farnsworth's voice came from under the couch in a whispery hiss that ended with a sob. "Where do you think the monster is hiding?"

To illustrate minimizing dialogue tags in a scene, here's an excerpt from a manuscript. In the scene, Marion Smith-Taylor, the U.S. Attorney General, is calling her office from out of town. See what you think, tag-wise.

Time enough for one last hail-Mary call—she opened her cell phone and auto-dialed her office. Suzanne Fisher answered. "Ms. Smith-Taylor's office, how may I help you?"

Marion pictured Suzanne, not in an office outfit but bundled up in her pale blue terry-cloth robe, blond hair tousled, fair cheeks flushed. If Marion had her druthers, Suzanne would be helping her to a tumbler of Scotch—but that would have to wait until she was home. "Hi, it's me."

"I was just thinking about you."

That was one of the things Marion loved about Suzanne—no coy games, she just said how she felt. "Me, too.

Listen, they're about to get here. Anything from Joe Donovan or Sally Arnold?"

"No word."

"Damn." She'd been praying for better information on the Oregon situation before the meeting. But she wasn't surprised; Joe and Sally had been less than helpful for months. Something had changed with them. "If you hear from them in the next hour, call."

"I will."

Maybe she'd have better luck on the other front that gave her sleepless nights, Oregon's constitution-busting new statute. Way under her radar, the so-called "Alliance" in Oregon had gotten over 250,000 signatures on a "Truth for Justice" initiative—twice what they needed. She'd been surprised when voters made it law, and now Oregon courts were forcing people to testify against themselves as if the Fifth Amendment didn't exist.

Marion said, "Connect me with Tiffany, okay?"

"Will you be back in time tomorrow for a quiet little supper at Angelo's?"

A candlelight dinner with Suzanne at their favorite restaurant sounded perfect—if only she were there now. "Should be. Make a reservation, eightish?"

Marion heard the smile in Suzanne's voice. "See you there. I'll get Tiffany for you now."

Thirteen speeches from two characters and just one dialogue tag. And I'll bet you didn't get lost.

Enough articulated?

What about "he thought?"—on using internal monologue

A common way of indicating the thoughts of a character are to signal with "he thought" and then include the thought in italics or use quotes.

But italics can be hard to read, quotes can lead to confusing thoughts with dialogue, and writing "he thought" isn't really necessary.

You can include a character's thoughts as a part of the narrative via internal monologue. Very simply, it's the thought expressed in the same person and tense as the rest of the narrative. For example, in this scene the protagonist, Jake, sees a woman being assaulted in an alley:

The woman staggered her attacker with a kick to his leg. He slapped her, and then had to dodge a knee aimed at his crotch. Girl had guts. Jake sighed, stepped into the alley, and drew his nine-millimeter Glock from the holster under his windbreaker.

"Girl had guts" is a snippet of internal monologue showing Jake's thought. It's a lot quicker and cleaner than this:

Jake thought, *the girl has guts.*

Here's a passage with a couple of instances of internal monologue from the woman who was being attacked. This happens after Jake intervenes and stops the attack. We're now in her point of view.

Jewel settled herself down. Her mama had always said, "In this world, you got to be hard. Ain't nobody there for you but you." Hallelujah, Mama.

She'd been lucky today. She felt compelled to thank the guy, even if he was white—Mama'd taught her manners, too. Jewel hurried after him, trying to arrange her torn top into decent coverage, but one tit or the other kept falling out. Great, now she had to walk down Michigan Avenue with her boobs hanging out. And wouldn't they love it back at the office.

Here, "Hallelujah, Mama" is internal monologue. And so is

Great, now she had to walk down Michigan Avenue with her boobs hanging out. And wouldn't they love it back at the office.

In *Self-editing for Fiction Writers*, authors Renni Browne and Dave King give a good example of this technique, which they call "interior monologue."

Big Jim Billups fondled the .38 in his pocket, waddled over to the back of his truck, and spat. Could've stopped the whole damn thing last night—they don't carry no guns. What was the use of doing a job if you didn't do a good one? He rocked, shifting his weight from one leg to another and spat again. The sound of the marchers was closer now. Soon it would be time.

As Browne and King point out, readers move easily from Big Jim's actions to his thoughts and back again without being aware of what they're doing. Renni and Dave's chapter on interior monologue gives excellent guidelines on the artful use of the technique.

> "I've read quite a few books on fiction writing, but have never seen this (absolutely vital) piece of nuts-and-bolts advice."
>
> "Niteowl," a Canadian writer

Dialogue

Cook up some tasty beats

Naked dialogue, just the speeches all by themselves, does only part of the job of delivering the experience of a scene. In life, and in fiction, dialogue doesn't happen in a vacuum—it happens in the midst of movement, body language, pauses for thought, and more. To bring dialogue to life, create "beats"— action interwoven with dialogue (including thought as action)—to invisibly accomplish a number of vital storytelling tasks, including:

➤ Advancing the story

➤ Increasing tension

➤ Illuminating character

➤ Identifying speakers without having to use dialogue tags

➤ Adding meaning to speeches that wouldn't otherwise be there

➤ Breaking up long strings of quotations to avoid a staccato effect and to create a pleasing rhythm

➤ Creating pictures in the reader's mind of what's going on (*Construe "picture" to include time [pace], scents, sensations, and sounds as well as action and physical description.*)

Here's an example of a beat that does one of those things…and yet is a waste of words. The scene is from a published novelist's first draft of a new story: a man and a woman sit at a table in a café, talking about a woman (his wife/her friend) who has been missing for over a week. In the course of the conversation in the woman's point of view, this happens:

A man from the next table asked to borrow the extra chair to my right. As I nodded, Robert said, "I have not told you everything."

"What?"

"Her car was found abandoned in Stewart State Park."

"Oh my God! When? How long after…"

The solo beat at the beginning did inject action into the scene…but it had nothing to do with story—it was "activity," not storytelling action. It didn't bear on the subject of the conversation, nor the people talking. It had no impact on the scene.

The dialogue that follows it suffers due to a lack of beats. How about a little body language when Robert confesses he hasn't told his listener everything? Or a reaction when the narrator learns fraught information?

Robert shifted his gaze away from me. "I have not told you everything."

How like the man to withhold information. "What?"

"Her car was found abandoned in Stewart State Park."

"Oh my God!" Fear for my missing friend jolted through me. "When? How long after…"

Here's what each of those beats accomplished:
- ➤ The first told you who was speaking and gave character and nuance to his speech.
- ➤ The second is internal monologue that adds characterization for both people.
- ➤ The last one injects emotion and more characterization.

Let's beat up some more dialogue. Here's part of a scene stripped naked, all of the beats removed. In this scene, KB, a law enforcement officer, reports to her superior, and she expects him to praise her for what she'd done the day before.

Captain Berman's door was open, as usual. KB tapped on the doorframe and went in.

"Take a seat, Lieutenant. So, you think you found a subject of interest."

"Yessir!"

"Did you see it with the thermal imaging device?"

"I did, sir."

"Did you record it?"

"Ah, no, sir."

"I see. You say it changed appearance on three occasions?"

"From a youngish woman to an older woman, then to a hick, then to a girl. Yessir."

"Did any of your team see these apparitions?"

"Schultz saw it come in. Sanchez saw it on the stairs, and Bailey saw it come out."

"After receiving your email, I asked your team for their input. Schultz didn't see a face."

"No, ah, he didn't get a good look. But he saw the glow in the camera."

"I see. No one else saw the older woman?"

"Not before she, uh, changed into a farmer."

You learn things, but there's no tension, no depth, you can't see a damn thing, and there's no rhythm—it's like a radio machine-gunning words at you. Now here's the full narrative—note one other thing while you're at it: there's not a single use of "said" or "asked" or any other dialogue tag in this narrative.

Captain Berman's door was open, as usual. His white-haired head was bent over a stack of paperwork, as usual. Adrenaline pumped her up, and she tapped on the doorframe and went in. The office was hot, as usual; the radiator must have been cranked all the way open.

He looked up and nodded. No smile. "Take a seat, Lieutenant."

The old fart was old-fashioned and formal, so maybe he was not gonna come right out with her attaboy. Sitting, she told herself to be patient, something that never came easily.

He signed a piece of paper, placed it in an out box, leaned back, laced his fingers over his belly, and gazed at her. "So, you think you found a subject of interest."

She smiled. "Yessir!"

"Did you see it with the thermal imaging device?"

Inside, she smirked at his fussy way of talking. "I did, sir."

"Did you record it?"

Oh, shit. She'd been too excited. "Ah, no, sir."

"I see." He leaned forward and studied a printout of her email. "You say it changed appearance on three occasions?"

"From a youngish woman to an older woman, then to a hick, then to a girl. Yessir."

"Did any of your team see these apparitions?"

Couldn't the old idiot read? "Schultz saw it come in. Sanchez saw it on the stairs, and Bailey saw it come out."

"After receiving your email, I asked your team for their input." He picked up a printout. "Schultz didn't see a face."

"No, ah, he didn't get a good look." Why did she feel like she was on trial? "But he saw the glow in the camera."

"I see." He read more. "No one else saw the older woman?"

"Not before she, uh, changed into a farmer."

The beats give pace to the conversation and much, much more. Through the beats you experienced:

➤ His chilly greeting when she expects warmth, and then his dawdling even though she is anxious (*finishing with papers, leaning back, lacing his fingers*)

➤ Her smugness (*the old fart was old-fashioned*)

➤ Her eagerness (*she smiled*)

➤ Her low opinion of him (*smirked at his fussy way of speaking to her*)

➤ Her realization of a mistake she's made (*too excited to record the suspect*)

➤ His calm, steady approach (*leaned forward and studied a printout*)

➤ More of her disrespect (*couldn't the old idiot read?*)

➤ His steady pursuit (*he picked up a printout and read it*)

➤ Her increasing anxiety (*was she on trial here?*)

You get a sense of escalating tension in KB. The scene continues to build from here, and ends with her feeling defeated, angry, and near tears when she'd begun the scene expecting praise. And it is the beats that take you there.

Not every line gets a beat—that'll wear a reader out. Every beat is tied to characterization and/or giving a picture of what is going on. The beats utilize physical action and internal monologue *(Couldn't the old idiot read?)* to add depth and context to the spoken words.

The beats help pace the exchange, creating pauses *(signed a piece of paper, placed it in an out box, leaned back, laced…)* and emphasis *(reading from something, etc.)*. Although there are no dialogue tags, you always know who's speaking and how they deliver their speeches.

The other cool thing about using beats is that it avoids the third most common dialogue flaw, explaining the dialogue with "with."

"I've read a lot of writing books and don't know of any that covered this subject as well as you did."

Ed Richbourg, writer

Dialogue
Don't say it with "with"

I have a pet peeve when it comes to a certain kind of description in dialogue. It's this type of statement:

> He gazed at the painting. "Marvelous," he said with satisfaction.

My feeling is that "he said with" construction signals lazy, ineffective dialogue. I went to *Self-Editing for Fiction Writers* by Renni Browne and Dave King to see what they have to say about it. While they didn't focus on the use of "with" in this way, it does fall within a craft no-no: explaining dialogue. Their position: don't do it. Mine, too.

For one thing, it's *telling*, not *showing*. The example above is just that—telling the reader what the character's emotion is, not showing the emotion.

Saying it with "with" is lazy writing because good dialogue shouldn't have to be explained. Both the words and the action surrounding it should show emotion and nuance.

What if the example above went something like this instead:

> He gazed at the painting, and then smiled. "Marvelous."

Written that way, I think the reader understands an even more complex array of emotion—pleasure, admiration, satisfaction—via the character's behavior without an iota of *telling*. Here are examples of "withage" from samples sent to me and from client manuscripts:

"Dialogue," she said with a huge grin.

Clumsy. You say things with your mouth, for one thing. Instead:

A grin stretched across her face. "Dialogue."

Note that you don't need a "she said" when you use an action beat in this way, although there's nothing wrong with a "she said" now and then if it helps the rhythm of your narrative.

"Dialogue," he said with such hope in his voice.

Nope. Show me with behavior that his emotion is one of great hope. What about this one?

"Dialogue," she said with a grin that couldn't help but make you smile back.

This is still "said with" and a complicated explanation of dialogue. What if it went this way?

She said, "Dialogue," and then flashed a grin that couldn't help but make you smile back.

There's more than a "said with" troubling the following narrative, including eyes that "dart" around.

"Dialogue," he said with his eyes darting around looking for hidden spies in the bushes.

Instead, how about:

His gaze darted over the bushes, looking for hidden spies. "Dialogue."

The following example tries to show me an attitude rather than tell me about it, but it's still driving in reverse.

"Dialogue," Farnsworth said with the assurance of a bridge player laying down the ace of trump.

Isn't his attitude clearer if you just turn it around?

With the assurance of a bridge player laying down the ace of trump, Farnsworth said, "Dialogue."

Come to think of it, "assurance" is still *telling*, isn't it? Wouldn't the reader get it if the narrative said this?

Like a bridge player laying down the ace of trump, Farnsworth said, "Dialogue."

Another aspect of "said with" is that it suggests that characters do things that are not really possible.

"Dialogue," he said with a shrug of his shoulders.

Unless you're using sign language, the only part of your body that actually says things is your mouth. When characters say things with a shrug or a scowl or a look, it bothers me.

By the way, the example also exhibits over-writing: the phrase "of his shoulders" is not needed. People don't shrug with any other part of their anatomy, and it suffices to say:

He shrugged. "Dialogue."

Note that a nine-word bit of narrative dropped to just three words, and became more effective.

Following are more real-life examples of using "said with" to explain dialogue. I've provided a blank line for you to make a note of how you would show the emotions instead of telling about them with "with."

It'll mean more if you actually do the rewriting.

"Dialogue," Steve said with contempt.

"Dialogue," I said with a bit of irritation in my voice.

"Dialogue," Ralph said with disgust.

"Dialogue," he said with obvious pride.

"Dialogue," Peggy said with a little belligerence.

"Dialogue," she said with delight.

"Dialogue," he said with a dull incurious inflection.

"Dialogue," he said with pretended anger.

"Dialogue," he said with seriousness befitting the formality.

Then there are the ones that try to blend action with speaking in ways that don't really work.

"Dialogue," she said with a giggle.

Not really. People giggle when they giggle and speak when they speak, but not at the same time. Instead, separate the action for a clearer picture and crisper dialogue.

She giggled. "Dialogue."

More examples from real manuscripts—in each case, think about how much more effective the dialogue portion would be if the action that characterizes it came first, and write your solution below it.

"Dialogue," Andrea said with her face screwed up.

_____

"Dialogue," Byron said with a sideways look at me.

_____

"Dialogue," she said with a wicked grin.

_____

"Dialogue," she said with a worried look.

_____

"Dialogue," she said with an admiring look.

_____

"Dialogue," he said with just the hint of a grin.

_____

"Dialogue," Susan said with a sigh.

_____

"Dialogue," Pete said with a chuckle in his voice.

_____

"Dialogue," she said with a frown.

_____

"Dialogue," he said with a fixed stare.

So, I say with determination, your dialogue will be far more effective if you show emotion rather than explain it, and place your illustrations before the dialogue so that the reader can apply the flavoring at the right time.

My advice? Search for "said with" and "asked with" and see if you can't do a better job of *showing* rather than *telling*.

Dialogue

How to deliver the sound of dialogue

What's wrong with this bit of narrative?

> "Hellooooo." The voice sounded ancient, an old lady maybe.

Description of the sound and character of a speech after it has happened is a subset of explaining dialogue. It may not be as obvious in a narrative, but I feel that it takes a step back from writing for effect, away from creating the experience of the action and dialogue in the reader's mind.

Maybe it's just me, but I feel that if you want a reader to experience how a character sounds or says a line, the clue has to come *before* the speech. When the description of the delivery comes after the fact, it's merely information. To have the experience, the reader would have to backtrack and re-imagine the speech, and no one does that—we're all moving forward to what happens next. In our example, you get closer to the experience if it's written this way:

> The woman's voice sounded ancient, maybe an old lady.
> "Hellooooo."

There's a bit of *telling* to think about with this example (taken from a real manuscript): what does "sounded ancient" really mean? As a reader, you have to interpret that, don't you? You have to call up what an "old" voice might sound like, and then fill in the blanks. But what if the writer had described the sound of the voice instead?

> The woman's voice rasped and quivered, maybe an old lady. "Hellooooo."

The "said with" construction we looked at earlier also creates, as my granny used to say, a "bassackward" effect because it *follows* a line of dialogue. For example:

> "Ants," he said with fear in his voice.

The reader needs to be shown the fear, not told, and before the speech:

> His eyes widened when black specks marched under the door, and his voice broke when he said, "Ants."

This gives the reader a chance of "hearing" the word "ants" with the speaker's abnormal delivery. A small point, perhaps, but a novel is made up of thousands of small points that either add up to the experience of the novel or just a compilation of information. For my money, you need to make every small point contribute to the experience.

Test your dialogue to see if:

- ➢ Your dialogue tags are either "said" or not there at all
- ➢ You include internal monologue and action beats that characterize or move the story forward
- ➢ You show the dialogue happening instead of explaining it with "with"
- ➢ You clue the reader to the sound of a speech before it happens

Section 4: Technique

In writing a novel, there are all kinds of things you have to know how to do. You need to know how to "show" a scene rather than "tell" it. On the other hand, there are times when "tell" is a better thing to do than "show." How's a writer to know?

And then there's point of view—first person, third person close, omniscient. Shifting the point of view in a narrative can be a great technique or a crummy one, depending on when and how you do it.

Motivating an action or a scene sometimes calls for setting it up many pages sooner—how do you avoid *deus ex machina?*

You worry about pace, about keeping things moving. . .is there ever a time you should slow down? The answer is yes.

Unless you want to your reader to become confused or lost, transitions need to be smooth and clear. And what about slipping into the past to show an important precursor to what's happening now?

This section covers:

- ➤ How to tell, when to show
- ➤ Point of view: a slippery slope
- ➤ Head-hopping as seen by an editor and an agent
- ➤ Story as garden
- ➤ Linger for involving storytelling
- ➤ From there to here, then to now
- ➤ The jump-cut transition
- ➤ Flashing back

> "While it'd be crazy to suggest that a writer's performance in the 'show don't tell' drill is what separates amateurs from Olympians, there's no doubt that internalizing Ray's wonderful encapsulation of the principle will improve the chances of a reader (like this grumpy editor, say) reading more than a single paragraph of your manuscript before tossing it on the scrap-heap."
>
> Mad Max Perkins, litblogger
> (aka Dan Conaway, Writers House literary agent,
> formerly executive editor at Penguin Putnam)

Technique

When to tell, how to show

In a recent edit, I pointed out instances where I felt my client was *telling* versus *showing*. Even though I included examples of ways to show what she had told, she wrote to me and said, "I'm not sure I know how to 'show' rather than 'tell'."

I can understand why. After all, we use the *telling* mode all the time in conversations with friends, and it works.

> "I was really surprised."
> "I was so pissed."
> "I was incredibly happy."

When to tell

There are times in a novel when *telling* is the right thing to do. It's when you need to summarize an event because to create a scene for it would be wrong in terms of pace, tension, etc. A common example is when you've shown an event in an earlier scene and then the story comes to a place where your character needs to pass along what happened to another character. Rather than drag your reader blow by blow through something she already knows, you just summarize:

> April told May how June had told Julie where to shove her opinion.

That's a necessary and effective use of *telling*.

There are other times when it's the best thing to do. For example, when what needs to happen is so mundane that to waste words on it is to waste words. For example, a character is talking on his cell phone. When he finishes the conversation, you could show this:

> Bob pressed the little blue phone icon on his cell-phone key-
> pad to end the call.

Truly, that wasn't needed and smacks of overwriting. Instead:

> Bob ended the call.

The reader can easily imagine ending a call with a cell phone if they've ever used one, and even if they haven't used one, they've seen it on television.

So what's so bad about a lot of *telling* in a novel? You "tell" a story, right? Not really. In a novel you *dramatize with scenes*. When you're writing for effect, you craft words that create a very specific result in the reader's mind, a vital sense of *what is happening*. You can only do that through *showing*.

Your readers want what they read to trigger in them the sights and sounds and smells of what's happening in the story. They don't want approximations, they don't want a report, they want to experience the story's reality.

How to show

You spot *telling* by looking for declarative sentences that tell the reader something. The verb "was" is often a sign of a telling statement.

Showing is using behavior (action, speech, thoughts) to illustrate or dramatize what the character is feeling/doing.

Here are looks at *telling* versus *showing* that come from actual writing samples.

The scene: Anna is beat from a long, bad day at work and now she's spent hours at the hospital with her father, who has been unconscious for days. You want to give the reader Anna's physical and emotional condition. This author wrote:

> Anna was physically and mentally exhausted.

Sure, you get information. You have an intellectual understanding of her condition. But you have no *feeling* for what Anna feels like, do you? To show that Anna is physically and mentally exhausted, you could write this:

> All Anna wanted to do was crawl into bed and go to sleep. But first she would cry. She didn't think she could be calm and composed for another minute.

The scene continues: Anna's father suddenly wakes and thrashes around wildly, gasping, making monitors go wild. You want to give the reader Anna's reaction. The author *told* us this:

> Anna was frightened.

She could have *shown* us with:

> Oh, God, what was happening? "Dad?" Why didn't he respond? "Nurse, do something!"

Yes, it takes more words, but remember that here you're not trying to inform the reader but to deliver an experience.

As you go through your manuscript, whenever you come across a "was-type" declarative sentence that simply delivers information rather than shows behavior, you probably have an instance of *telling*.

Your task then is to visualize the character in that state or situation. See the movie. As the author, you can also "hear" thoughts. Then *show* the reader the thinking or speaking or moving in a way that illustrates what the reader needs to know.

Another example, one that deals with the use of adverbs.

> *Telling:* He stabbed the man furiously.

See how an adverb tells rather than shows?

> *Showing:* He plunged the dagger into the man's chest again and again and again, screaming "Die!" each time the blade stabbed into flesh.

One more example. Jesse has been working for hours under the Texas sun. We need to let the reader know how he feels.

Telling: Jesse was very hot.

Seriously, I see descriptions like that in manuscripts all the time. How about this?

Showing: Jesse felt like an overcooked chicken, his meat damn near ready to fall off his bones.

Now, that's *hot*. Another thing I often see is where a writer does a good job of *showing*, but then feels compelled to add an explanation (*telling*). From a recent edit:

He wrenched her from the quicksand with a last huge pull and fell back onto the ground, panting as if he'd just won a wrestling match, temporarily drained by the supreme effort.

For my money, "as if he'd just won a wrestling match, temporarily drained by the supreme effort" has already been shown by his panting and the effort he put into the rescue, so it's redundant and repetitive. I would delete it.

Boiled down to essentials:
➤ *Telling* is dispensing information.
➤ *Showing* is evoking experience.

With each word and phrase you write, slip into reader mode and see what the effect is: is it just informing you, or bringing to life what the character experiences?

"The most understandable and then applicable example I have seen."

Patti Tucker
English instructor
Pennsylvania State University

> "Little by little, your teachings lay themselves down, rather like autumn leaves falling in the midst of a silent forest, to make their quiet home in my brain."
>
> Mai Liadan, writer

Technique

Point of view: a slippery slope

Point of view [POV] is the perspective from which a writer tells a story. There are three basic categories. Lynn Viehl, author of forty novels in five genres, gave these examples on her blog, *Paperback Writer*:

1. *First person* (the story is told from the perspective of **I** or **We**):

I grabbed Marcia's arm. "What was that about my wallpaper?"

2. *Second person* (the story is told from the perspective of **You**), generally in present tense:

You grab Marcia's arm and demand she repeat the crack she made about your wallpaper.

3. *Third person* (the story is told from the perspective of **He, She, It** or **Them**):

John grabbed Marcia's arm. "What's wrong with my wallpaper?"

Much of modern fiction is written in the close third person point of view, which means the story as experienced by a character, from "inside" the character's head. Many of the writers whose work I see try to do that. But they often "slip" in subtle ways.

To maintain a close third person point of view, the narrative contains nothing that a character CANNOT directly see, hear, taste, feel, or know. In other words, just like you and me in real life.

> When we're talking with someone, we can't know what they're thinking—unless they tell us.

> When we see someone do something, we can't know their motive or purpose—unless they tell us.

> If we're asleep or knocked unconscious or shot dead, the narrative in our point of view can't then show what happens to us. (I have seen this happen in manuscripts.)

Now, there are actually no "rules" in fiction, so writers can and do stray from this guideline all the time. But there can be negative results if you don't keep a consistent point of view.

Consider why you might want a close third person point of view. It's to involve your reader with your protagonist. To create an emotional bond, some form of caring. If the reader cares about a character, they're a whole lot more likely to care about what happens next. And thus motivated to turn the page.

More than that, the closer you can bring a reader to a character, the tighter the emotional connection and involvement, and the closer you bring a reader to *experiencing* the story rather than just reading information.

If that's true, then slipping away from the close third person has the effect of distancing the reader from a character. Of taking her out of the mind and heart of the protagonist. Of disconnecting.

I want to show you some POV slips that occurred in writing samples that have been sent to me. They seem innocuous, but I believe they have their effect.

Perhaps at first glance there's nothing wrong with this narrative.

She felt radiant, and her brown eyes glistened with happy tears.

Here's the slip:

She felt radiant, and *her brown eyes glistened* with happy tears.

Because we're in the woman's point of view, she *can't see her eyes glisten*. That's impossible unless she's looking into a mirror, and she's not.

From a storytelling point of view, the reader is forced a step back from the character. Because only from *outside* the character's point of view can it be perceived that her brown eyes glisten.

She can't see it so, if it is seen, it has to be from the outside. Maybe an arm's length away? One other thing that's a point of view glitch—mentioning the color of her eyes. While she certainly knows the color of her eyes, who ever thinks about the color of their eyes when they're crying? Not me. Not anyone.

Okay, then how do you get images across without stepping out of her point of view? Well, in the first case you can say something such as "tears welled in her eyes." True, we don't *say* glistening, but the reader knows what tears in eyes look like. Basically, all the writer is trying to do here is show the reader that the character is tearing.

I know this seems like a small thing, but the effect is cumulative. "Her brown eyes glistened" is the author's point of view, and that pulls the reader out of the identification with the character that is so necessary for making a reader care about what happens enough to want to keep reading.

While we're here, let me dwell a moment on the use of "felt" in this description. I know that there are times when you must use that verb—I have—but it borders on *telling*. If it's possible to describe the sensation in a more active way, I think it's better. For example, instead of "felt radiant," what if "joy filled her"?

Here's another POV slip where the author intrudes. It's from within the head of a bad guy—with the "evil presence" he is referring to himself.

> Stephenson looked down on the woman who slept unaware of the evil presence standing only yards from her tranquil slumber.

Because we're in Stephenson's point of view, he would not be standing there thinking of himself as an "evil presence." This is the author intruding, to characterize him. I don't think bad guys go around thinking of themselves as evil. Sound motivation for antagonists gives them the point of view that they're doing the right or necessary thing, not something for purposes of evil.

What about this one?

> She fell to the floor, her eyes wide and panicked.

Yes, this is a subtle, tiny thing. But we're supposed to be *inside* her head. Where do you have to be in order to see if someone's eyes are wide and panicked? Standing next to them, right? Unless she's standing next to herself, she can't see what her eyes look like.

The author is doing the right thing in terms of trying to use action to convey emotion, and the description does that. But it's emotion as perceived from *outside* the character, not inside.

Here's another little one:

> George spoke in a calm voice.

This characterization of his voice is as perceived from outside the character's mind, as heard by an objective observer. True, you can make a character aware of what his voice sounds like, e.g., "His voice sounded calm to his ears." But that's not what this author has done here.

So how can this writer get "calm voice" across without stepping out of point of view? One method is the one above, where he is listening to the quality of his voice. But that wasn't the intent of this narrative. It was to communicate the way the character was delivering his words. From inside the character's mind, it would be something like:

> George kept his voice calm.

POV Peeves

I have two pet peeves about point of view [POV] that I frequently see in the narratives of both unpublished and published authors:

1. Failing to maintain a steady POV
2. "Head-hopping" from one point of view to another.

I say no hops, skips, or jumps without some kind of transitional element. When you're in a POV, you should STAY in it. When I come upon POV slips, even little ones, they always pull me out of the story.

Inconsistent POV

Here's an example from a published novel. In a two-sentence paragraph that follows the revelation of shocking news to the character, Smith, the first sentence is this:

> Smith felt his head go light.

Other than that the writer used "felt" instead of illustrating this feeling, we're in a very close (limited) third person point of view, right inside the guy's head. Now I'll add the second sentence:

> Smith felt his head go light. Unaware of the action, he moved his free hand over his heart and clutched at his breast.

WHAM! We vault from inside the guy's head to a Godlike, omniscient POV to see action the character doesn't know is happening. For my money, any limited point of view means writing ONLY about what the character perceives, does, feels, says, etc. If he or she doesn't perceive it, it doesn't belong in that portion of the narrative. If this character is unaware of what the hand is doing, it should not be included.

One writer I know continued with the action after he had killed the point-of-view character, who could hardly be aware of what was happening around his corpse.

Worse, in the published example above, "Unaware of the action" refers to the lightening of the character's head in the preceding sentence rather than the hand. Ba-a-ad structure. This is from a "bestselling" author, too.

Don't you just hate it when you see published writing that's less skillful than your own?

Were I editing this, I'd suggest the writer get rid of "unaware of the action." It serves no purpose, the picture of the action works without it, and it points to the previous action.

I would also advise this writer to look for some way besides the verb "felt" to describe the feeling the character has. Felt is a passive, lazy verb that doesn't do much for picturing. Part of the way I edit is to provide suggestions to illustrate craft points. In this case, I might suggest something like:

> Smith's mind seemed to detach and drift, and his hand clutched at his heart.

Second look: the hand part is passive. Why not this?

> Smith's mind seemed to detach and drift, and he clutched at
> his heart.

Maintaining a solid point of view is tricky at times, and we all make these little slips, especially in a first draft when we're just trying to get the story on the page.

So keep an eye out for places where it's you, the author, seeing things and reporting on them instead of your character experiencing them *from inside*. The closer you keep a character's point of view, the better your chances of involving your reader more and more deeply.

Head-hopping

When you use an omniscient [third-person] point of view, it is appropriate to skillfully move from one character's point of view to another's. The catch is "skillfully." If you're Virginia Woolf, you'll do fine. Richard Russo, novelist, screenwriter, and lecturer at the Warren Wilson College MFA Program for Writers, writes that using omniscience is a mature writer's technique — he didn't attempt it until he was forty.

The omniscient approach, used well, doesn't seek to imitate the close third person technique. The trouble comes when a writer uses the close third person POV from character to character to character, shifting from inside one head to inside another at will and with no transition.

Here's an example from the published novel we just looked at. At this point, the author has been using Smith's close third person point of view for several pages. The paragraph below is tightly inside Smith's point of view, in his head.

> Smith knew that this meant the suspect would probably
> wind up going to the hospital. The idea didn't much appeal
> to him. "Get him in a cell."

So far, so good. Now for the following paragraph. I'll repeat the first for contrast.

> Smith knew that this meant the suspect would probably
> wind up going to the hospital. The idea didn't much appeal
> to him. "Get him in a cell."

Jones shrugged. It wasn't that he cared, but Smith's suggestion ran counter to protocol.

He wanted to cover himself. "Clear him here first, then."

Whoa. We went from knowing what Smith knows and feels about an idea directly into what Jones feels and desires. Mental whiplash for this reader. Again, this blatant head-hopping occurred after many pages that had held tightly to Smith's point of view. For me, sloppy, undisciplined writing (or editing). As it happens, Jones was a minor character who disappeared in a sentence or two anyway, so I have to wonder why the author felt the need to include what he felt and wanted. In an edit, I'd have cut all but the dialogue, and maybe suggested some visualization of Jones's discomfort from Smith's point of view—but no interior monologue.

What's the harm in this? I believe that, at some level, head-hopping reduces/damages/breaks the emotional bond the writer has worked so hard to create by being in the close third person. Why? Because the hand of the author is clearly revealed and the reader, either consciously or somewhere down under, feels the manipulation of an external force, which is contrary to being carried along with what's happening to the character she's involved with. The emotional effect of the narrative is diminished and, as Sol Stein says, creating emotion in a reader is the author's job.

Technique

Head-hopping as seen by publishing pros

You see plenty of head-hopping in published works, and I wondered if I was taking the wrong stance in being so critical of it. So I surveyed a number of New York publishing pros—editors and agents—for their views.

An executive editor's view of head-hopping

I share your peeve about "head-hopping"—apt term. So thanks for letting me blather on about it.

I think it's OK to do it so long as there is only one point of view per *discernible section*. [RR: emphasis mine.] That is to say, so long as there's something to represent to the reader that there has been some kind of jump. A chapter or a space break or something.

But when it happens in the middle of continuous action, it's a serious problem. Basically, if you tell your story with recourse to everyone's head at all times, you're basically throwing out all the rules and permitting yourself everything. And if you are permitting yourself everything, then you also forfeit the right to hide anything of narrative importance—who the killer is, for instance—without cheating in a major way.

I've always tried to tell the writers that I work with that some kind of consistency of point of view—some ground rules that the reader can grasp—is an essential element of what is an epistemological problem. How does the reader know what he knows? Of course the author knows everything in advance—after all, he came up with the story. But he has to maintain the illusion that the reader and the narrative are on the same footing, discovering at the same time what the author has cooked up. After all, once the reader knows everything, the narrative is over.

Mystery stories are great examples of this kind of narrative epistemology. I always pointed out to the writers I worked with that all the Sherlock Holmes tales were narrated in the first person and by Holmes's friend, for very sound reasons. Had Doyle used third person, a reader might well ask, "If you are employing the omniscient narrator, then you know everything, including the killer's identity. In which case you should tell us!" Whereas by using Dr. Watson, he shields himself from this accusation. Dr. Watson can't possibly know the outcome in advance, and so he reports on the action and shares with the reader the process of discovery. Watson knows enough to introduce Holmes to the reader, but once the story starts, he knows as much as the reader does.

With the advent in the twentieth century of close third person, the objection on the basis of omniscience is less relevant. A writer can use a kind of limited omniscience narrative. And I think that's OK. Provided nothing is hidden. Agatha Christie used to use a Dr. Watson-like device for her Poirot novels, but then got rid of it, no doubt when she realized that simply following Poirot in close[-enough] third person was sufficient.

Still, that doesn't excuse her gross violation of this principle in *The ABC Murders*, where she expands her omniscience but nonetheless hides crucial elements from the reader merely as a ploy to keep the mystery going.

So I think it's very important, in head-hopping, to keep the points of view distinct through the use of clearly demarked boundaries—space breaks, chapters, etc.—and also to make sure that each point of view is seen divulging the entirety of its knowledge of the narrative.

[RR: Rather than "head-hopping," I think of this approach as "point-of-view shifts." The former involves sudden, unrestricted, unmotivated jumps in the midst of action while the latter uses clearly signaled breaks limited to reasonably long, discreet segments of narrative.]

Nonetheless, I do see many bestselling works of fiction that practice 'head-hopping' in continuous action, and no one seems to care. Well, not 'no one,' but nearly—I thought I was it until your email came along.

Perhaps in terms of encouraging writers, it's best to focus on what consistency in use of point of view can deliver, and get away from what it's meant to avoid. The masterpieces of unreliable narration, from *The Aspern Papers* to *The Remains of the Day*—not to mention Ron Howard's adaptation of *A Beautiful Mind*—all attest to the power of point of view. In other words, don't make point of view just a vehicle of narrative, make it a partner, or a driving force, in narrative.

I've a client who, when I pointed out how much she hopped from head to head, told me that head-hopping was common in her romance sub-genre. Yet I know an editor with a firm that publishes romance who hates head-hopping—and summarily rejects novels that do it.

A top New York literary agent wrote to say

I am in absolute agreement with you. People do it, but, for the most part, it doesn't work (I'm not going to say never, because this is fiction we're talking about, not algebra). "Hopping," as you've put it, distances the reader from the close emotional connection with the central point-of-view character in the scene, it draws attention to the fact that writing is an artifice (destroying the "suspension of disbelief" that reading a novel usually though not always entails), and it generally just plain sounds awkward. Unless it's masterfully pulled off, it usually signals a lack of control of authorial voice, to my mind.

On the other hand, an editor at a major New York imprint opined,

I am not overly troubled by rotating POV if the writer can sustain the variety of voices and allow the reader to maintain clarity in his/her mind about who is whom. Singular POV is not sacrosanct, in my opinion.

Here, though, because he uses the term "rotating," I think the editor is actually talking about skillful use of multiple points of view, not bolting from head to head within a scene. By the way, Donald Maass suggests that ending a chapter at a moment of suspense and then shifting to another point of view for the next chapter is a good way to build tension.

As with just about anything in writing long-form fiction, there aren't really any rules. However, I don't think there's an agent or editor who has a problem with a consistent, "non-hoppy" narrative, so why take the chance of (a) running into someone who hates it, and (b) distancing your reader from your characters?

Here's something on the subject I found on English teacher and author Crawford Kilian's the *Fiction Writer's Page* website that describes "episodically limited third-person omniscient POV," a single close third-person narrator. He also describes using the POV character's voice as the narrator as I suggest for characterizing each character's narrative.

> Whoever is the point of view for a particular scene determines the persona. An archbishop sees and describes events from his particular point of view, while a pickpocket does so quite differently. So the narrator, in a scene from the archbishop's point of view, has a persona quite different from that of the pickpocket: a different vocabulary, a different set of values, a different set of priorities. As a general rule, *point of view should not change **during** a scene*. [emphasis mine] So if an archbishop is the point of view in a scene involving him and a pickpocket, we shouldn't suddenly switch to the pickpocket's point of view until we've resolved the scene and moved on to another scene.

Maintaining a consistent point of view within a scene is the best craft, but a novelist can change point of view within scenes if clearly differentiated and integrated. In a fast-action scene involving characters the reader knew well, I used this technique to create a whole with their separate parts:

> Marion screamed. The woman turned toward her and shot.
> The bullet slammed into Marion's neck—
>
> • • •
>
> Karl watched Marion fall. It seemed like slow motion.
> This couldn't be real.
> He ran down the aisle toward her.

Technique

Story as garden

While enjoying one of my favorite films, *The Abyss*, I was reminded of the need for effective "seeding" of character and action. The film does it well.

At one point a roughneck in the crew holds up his massive fist and tells a buddy that "they used to call this the hammer." That nicely sets up a time later in the film when he knocks a bad guy head over keister with one mighty punch. Because of the setup, it was absolutely credible. (Well, the guy's size was a part of that, too.)

Another fine setup had to do with the hero's wedding ring as a life-saving device. After a spat between Bud and Lindsey, his about-to-be-divorced wife (and the heroine), he throws his wedding band in a toilet. He leaves. Comes back and fishes the ring out. Cut to extreme close-up of wedding band going back on his finger.

While at the time this seemed pointed at characterizing him and his feelings about her—and it was—that wasn't everything it did. Later in the film the hold he is in is flooding. He dashes for an already-closing hatch door and manages to put a hand into the gap. Ordinarily his hand would have been crushed by the hydraulic door, but it's not. Yep, his wedding ring stops the door from closing all the way. Rescuers come and the door is opened. But that must have been one helluva wedding ring.

Without the setup, the ring-stopping-the-door trick would have been a mini *deus ex machina* and a laughable coincidence. These "seedlings" in the film work so well because they don't call attention to themselves and just seem like normal parts of what's happening. Thank you, excellent screenwriter, for your good gardening.

A mystery writer must, of course, plant clues—interesting how even the language for doing this kind of thing is from gardening—but the rest of us need to pay attention to our seeding as well, for both action and characterization.

In a romance novel I recently edited, almost at the end of the book the heroine is groped from behind in a public place by a man whom she assumes to be her current love. She goes along with it because they've made love in risky places before. Unfortunately, it's her old lover doing the groping. As bad luck would have it, her current guy bursts in on the scene. Despite her sincere explanations, he goes into a jealous snit and declares that the relationship won't work. Goodbye.

When Hairball saw Shedder nuzzle Barfie, he flew into a rage

All good grist for the romance mill…but for one thing. The current guy has been Mister Adoring Puppy the whole way. He has accepted her dalliance with a celebrity in the beginning of the relationship, including a hot sleepover. He has been accommodating in every way, constantly declaring his love with words and actions. That's another thing I talked to the writer about—the guy is just too perfect. No flaws. No character arc. No contention between him and her except for the before-mentioned snit.

The problem with how he reacted to this incident was that the motivation for a strong jealous reaction had never been set up. To react strongly was out of character for this guy. Luckily, it didn't have to be, and I was able to suggest to the writer how to fix it by drawing on other material already in the story. It seems that the protagonist's first love was jealous and, whenever she even spoke to another man, he would put his arm around her and interfere. If the writer has Mr. Perfect do something similar (an action to which she can react, thereby inserting even more characterization for her) and exhibit a bit of jealousy, then his motive for the later scene will be established and it will be credible.

"Post-seeding"

Computers are wonderful in the way they give you the ability to go back and change things in the earlier pages of a novel quickly and easily when a late thought creates the need for seeding a development in your story. Here's an example of "post-seeding."

About a third of the way into a novel, the female protagonist needs to be pulled out of a suicidal dive caused by the tragic death of her once-in-a-lifetime love. She encounters a small boy who seems to suffer from autism.

She is a healer, and is sympathetic, but his condition and innocence didn't seem like motive enough to stir her from her depression.

So what would? How about if the child reminded her in a specific, powerful way of the man she had loved and lost? So the author went back to the scene leading to her love's death and gave him a "little-boy-lost" look that had always melted her heart. Then the narrative showed her seeing that same look in the eyes of the boy. That stimulus started her on the path of helping the child, which ultimately brought her back to emotional life. The phrase "little-boy-lost" was seeded in three places that added up to powerful motivation for her when the right time came. By the way, the seed had to be distinctive enough to be easily recalled when the time came; in this case, little-boy-lost not only fit unobtrusively the first time it was used, i.e., didn't call attention to itself, it was distinct enough to remember later.

So seed your novel with small things early on that grow to be significant. And don't hesitate to go back and plow up early ground to plant the antecedents of characters and events that come into being in the process of discovering your story.

Technique

Linger for involving storytelling

I took a course in literary manuscript development at the University of Washington from novelist Laura Kalpakian. She gave my storytelling high marks for dialogue, description, and pace—but she didn't get enough from my narrative about the characters to truly involve her, to make her care. For her, my narrative was simply too lean at times for her to experience what was happening to the character in a way that connected with her.

Her wise advice: "Linger."

The following paragraph comes from a writer's sample that I critiqued in my blog. In the scene, a teenage boy is approaching a girl's home for his first date with her, and he's never been there.

> Her mother opened the door as he approached. "Come right in. Kathy isn't ready yet; it'll be just a minute." He found himself in the living room with her mother, father, and little brother. He tried not to say much, passing the time, trying to get through the ordeal without coming apart.

In this writer's haste to get the boy and girl out the door and to their date, he's missed opportunities to draw the reader into the boy's story and build sympathy for his character, not to mention create tension and story questions about what's going to happen. Anybody who's been a teenage boy calling on a girl for the first time knows how tense the situation and the boy are. The narrative would be far better served with a brief scene instead of the summary done here. For example, just one of the rich possibilities to explore in a scene is the look the father gives the boy (for he would give him a look, I'm certain), and the boy's perception/reaction to it.

> Kathy's father lowered his bushy brows and gave Jimmy a look that made him feel like he was lying under an X-ray machine. He jerked a quick little smile and blurted, "Pleased to meet you, sir." Then he realized how stupid that was because nobody had actually introduced them. The sweat under his arms cranked up to a steady drip.

I would linger more in that living room to capture character and build tension. In this writer's manuscript, all too quickly he had the teenagers escape the girl's house and go to a dance in the high school gym. When they dance close, she gives signals of interest such as pressing tightly against him, and he becomes aroused. When they leave the dance, the writer gives us this:

> At twelve, he guided Kathy to their coats and out into the frosty October air. The car heater kicked in nicely as they drove down Main Street and into the countryside. The farms they passed were dark. Jamie turned down a gravel road and slowed.

The night is frosty, but what else is there when they walk out of that gym? There's no tension or anticipation in this expository paragraph, but great opportunity to build it. Is there a moon out? Mightn't he gaze at her face and have some romantic/lusty thoughts as he takes her to the car? If it's like any high school dance I ever went to back in the day, there are kids outside, some smoking, some necking. For example, what if we lingered just a bit like this?

> At midnight, he guided Kathy to their coats and out into the frosty October air. Laughter and the sweet aroma of cigarette smoke wafted from three guys huddled beside a pickup truck. When Jimmy and Kathy passed a parked car with steamed-up windows, he heard thumping and the car rocked on its springs. He glanced at Kathy and found her gazing at the car. If only...

She looked up at him and grinned. She tiptoed and leaned against him to whisper into his ear, pressing her belly against his hand. "I don't have to be home until one."

Oh, man…

That little bit of description and action didn't take many words, but you get a greater sense of place and time, and the sexual tension between the two is ramped up. As a result, the coming necking and petting when they park will be that much more meaningful.

Stay with scenes long enough to enrich them with "story meaning"—character emotions and reactions to settings and happenings that deepen the reader's understanding and connection.

Lingering means:

➢ Take the time to let your characters come to life on the page.

➢ Bring them to life with action that characterizes and advances the story.

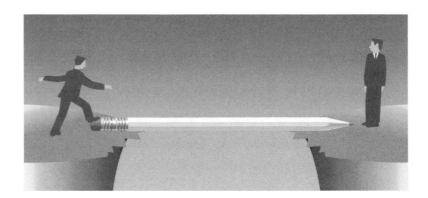

Technique

From there to here, then to now

Often in an edit I'll see a need for a transition. Writers sometimes just leap over time and space without giving the reader a clue as to what's going on. This is caused, I suspect, by the usual syndrome—the writer sees all in his/her head but just doesn't get it on paper.

So how do you get from there to here…or from then to now? I advocate using character and action. The following example is a simple shift from one location to another; such a transition, in a book, would include a blank line between paragraphs like this to denote a change in place or time.

> Jennifer knew there was only one place to find Jason. She raced out the door and down the stairs to the parking garage.

> As soon as Jennifer hit the smoky air in Timothy's Tavern it hit right back—eyes, throat, lungs. God, how could Jason stand this?

What the reader will know without being told:
- ➤ Jennifer drove to the tavern (she raced to her parking garage).
- ➤ She is inside the tavern (so must have parked her car and come in the door).

Note how the transition is motivated by action that leads the reader to expect movement.

What isn't needed because it has no impact on the story:
- ➤ Getting Jennifer into her car
- ➤ Showing Jennifer driving down Main Street and taking a hard left on Pine.
- ➤ Slamming the door of her car and racing across the parking lot at Timothy's Tavern.
- ➤ Opening the door to Timothy's Tavern and running in.

Here's an example from my edit files of a narrative that needs transitional work. It's from a paranormal romance. I'll give it to you straight, then with my comments.

> She slowed her breathing and reached for the deep sleep. Instinctively, her mind connected with Randall's. Together, they drifted into sleep. Their breath left their bodies at the same time. Their hearts stopped beating as one.
>
> Randall stared at the faces gathered before him. Some of them were good friends, others were mortal enemies. He took a deep breath and said firmly, "I've called this Council today to introduce my intention to take a mate."

It's not my job, as an editor, to create a transition for an author—but it is my job to point out the need and make suggestions. Here, along with a little line editing and comments (italicized), is what I did:

> She slowed her breathing and reached for the deep sleep. Instinctively, her mind connected with Randall's. Together, they drifted into sleep. ~~Their breath left their bodies at the same time.~~ Their hearts stopped beating as one.

* * *

(I added a line space and asterisks to indicate changes in point of view and scene.)

> Randall stared at the faces gathered before him. *(A little transition and scene-setting would be good. Even "the next night" would help. What time of the day/night is it? Where are they? How many council members? What are the attitudes emanating from them? Is Randall on his throne? "Faces" suggests a clump of people standing before him? Are they? Or are they sitting in chairs? Around a table? What?)* Some were good friends, others mortal enemies.

(Technically, "faces" can't be friends or enemies. How about: Some of them belonged to good friends, others to mortal enemies.) He took a deep breath and said ~~firmly~~, "I've called this Council today to introduce my intention to take a mate."

There are times an author, lost in the fullness of her understanding of the story, shortchanges the reader on the transition from time to time, place to place, or person to person. I'm sure you've had the disorienting experience of sailing along in a narrative only to suddenly become lost when the story-teller vaults to an unexpected somewhere/when/one else.

Transitions can—and often should—be simple and virtually unnoticeable. At other times, they are a valuable tool for enriching the story by characterizing through description or action.

Here are a couple of examples from manuscripts I've edited.

From here to there

We start with the character in her bedroom:

> I lie back down, but there's no chance of me going back to sleep now, so I get up and put the kettle on. As I sit down with a cup of tea, Amy appears.

I was okay with this through putting the kettle on, but then. . . Where does she sit down? In her room? In the kitchen? If it's in the kitchen, the writer needs to transition her, to locate her there for the reader. Perhaps dress her—when she rises, does she put on a robe or clothes? What are they? And tell us if there are sounds of other arousal in the flat, if anyone is in the kitchen or it is blessedly empty, etc. Let us see her in action.

Another "here to there" slip—the characters are in a bedroom:

> With no more than a thought, he dressed them both for the banquet. Alex looked down at the beautiful crimson gown and reached up to feel her intricately done hair. Damien's power was so easy to him, so effortless. It was one more difference between the two of them.
>
> Alex said, "I'm going back to my old room, Damien."
>
> "You will not," Damien said, his voice steely. "You will cease this foolishness right now. You forget who is master here." He grabbed her arm.

He was interrupted by a vampyress who came sailing out of the banquet to catch his arm. Alex eyed the beautiful vampyress and the possessive way she took Damien's arm.

In this case, the author was so eager to get to the coming conflict at the banquet she forgot to transport us there. The fix could be as simple as adding a line break after the first paragraph—before Alex's dialogue—and a snippet of transition:

. . .It was one more difference between the two of them.

Just outside the banquet room, Alex said, "I'm going back to my old room…"

From time to time

In another novel, we're at a cockfight, and the roosters have been set loose:

They danced at first, happy to be on their feet as if they'd kiss, but then something within them said "KILL" and they lunged like Spartans with green head feathers, short-handled daggers and form-fitting breast plates. Oooh's and ahh's followed every thrust and bend. Feathers floated away from wounds like wishes from dandelions. Screams and battle-cry cackles sounded out pain and laughter.

The sight of the loser went right through me. A beaten soldier on the battlefield after the last bayonet strike. Lying limp and shaking, pecked to near death, eyes out, broken wings, wounds gaping.

If the writer is going to jump to the end of the fight, we need a time transition. First, an extra line space between the paragraphs is a customary—and useful—way to indicate a gap in time. In manuscript form, adding a centered "#" helps clue in the reader, though it may not be needed in printed form.

In this case, I don't even know how long one of these matches lasts. Minutes? An hour? A transition and some information would be good. For instance, even something such as "Twenty bloody minutes later, the sight of the loser went right through me" would do wonders for the reader.

From person to person

Transitions between characters can be simple or complex. The following example moves from one character to another within a chapter, but carefully—in my view, head-hopping should be avoided at all costs.

This transition uses a line break/centered asterisks convention to signal shifting from one point of view to another. But it takes more than that to make the shift seamless and effortless. Here, the action of one character is tied to the other so the scene seems to flow continuously even though there is a point-of-view break.

She mounted the steps and came upon a slender man in a black overcoat. The man aimed a small video camera her way. As she turned her face away, she saw his lips move, and the wind carried his words to her.

He said, "I think I got one."

She looked behind her. Nothing of interest there. Shielding her face with her scarf, she shifted her gaze to the man, and he jerked the camera away. She believed that he wanted to conceal his purpose.

But what did it matter? It could have nothing to do with her.

* * *

"I think I got one." The whisper shivered in KB Volmer's earpiece. She stepped out of the gallery of art done by kids in Ireland. It hadn't looked any better than the stuff her mother had taped on the refrigerator when she was a kid.

Speaking just loudly enough for her collar mike to pick up her words, she said, "Again."

"I got one."

Tying two characters' actions together in this way also works when moving from the end of a chapter to the beginning of the next.

The jump-cut transition

Sometimes no transition at all is the way to go if you can use jump cuts to collapse time for powerful pacing.

In film, "jump cuts" are often used to collapse time. The moniker is literal—in the midst of a scene the action jumps ahead from one moment to one further down the timeline rather than following all of the action as it happens. The technique accelerates pace and can enhance the impact of the action.

Jump cuts work in fiction, too, but care has to be taken with setting the scene. In a film, the viewer has a complete picture given to him at all times. In fiction, we have to supply it. And that's where I see writers missing the mark.

Chapters are a great opportunity for jump cuts. You can end a chapter or scene in one place, wrapping up an action and setting up a future course, and then jump to a completely different scene…*as long as you fill the reader in on what that new scene is.*

Here's an example. The heroine, Ailia, has been arrested by Homeland Security and a rogue agent has used torture tactics that could take her life. The action takes place in Chicago in the midst of winter, and the reader has been freezing along with the character in this chapter. She has escaped her holding cell and. . .

> She dashed to the doorway marked Exit and hurtled down the stairs.

We next see the character in the Florida Everglades. In real time, she would need to leave the building, go to O'Hare Airport, buy a ticket, get on a plane, land elsewhere, rent a vehicle, and travel. Ho hum. Instead, here's the jump cut to the opening of a new chapter:

> Eager to see the ships of her clan, Ailia peered ahead as she steered an airboat through saw-grass marsh deep within the three million acres of the Everglades.
>
> The warm air coddled her, such a relief from the energy drain of keeping warm in Chicago. Sunset colored the sky with bands of pink and mauve. A silhouetted heron winged past, grace in motion. After traveling all night and most of the day, she relished the idea of coming to rest.

The first sentence, a mere twenty-eight words, quickly transports the character to a place a thousand miles away. Note that it does so from *within* her point of view, giving the reader a sense of character through her reactions to where she is and at the same time enabling the reader to "see" the character's surroundings.

The story's other primary protagonist, Gabe, was also captured and tortured by the agent. He was broken out from his cell by the Drago character you've met before. Gabe and Ailia are destined to travel very different paths before they are reunited. Here's Gabe's escape scene.

> Drago opened a door to a stairwell. "Quickly, others may come."
> Gabe followed him up toward the roof. What did Drago have up there, a helicopter? A magic broom? It didn't matter to Gabe, anything to get away from people determined to torture and kill him.

So they go into the night. The story calls for Gabe to go with Drago to his home place, which would involve climbing the stairs, getting onto the vehicle Drago has on the roof, and traveling across Chicagoland in the dark to a forest preserve. But that's not action that will move the plot along. So, at the beginning of Gabe's new chapter, we jump:

> A moan broke Gabe free from a nightmare and he bolted upright. It had been his voice, a teeth-clenched cry forced out by a vision of himself frozen upright, white with frost, arms reaching for his son but doomed to never embrace him.
> A quilt fell from him and cold air struck his bare torso. The bed was a bunk fastened to a paneled wall. The room wasn't much more than sleeping quarters, maybe six feet by eight. There was space enough in a corner for an antique-looking washstand and an old-fashioned pitcher in a large bowl. Neatly folded, a small towel and washcloth waited next to it. His shirt and jeans were draped over a single chair. Reddish sunlight glowed through a porthole.
> A porthole?

So we're off and running in a new place that is clearly very strange to Gabe, experiencing it from within his point of view.

When you jump cut, make sure you give the reader solid footing when he lands so that he knows where he is. Do it from within the character's experience so description becomes part of the action, not simple exposition.

Technique
Flashing back

Flashbacks are risky. You chance losing readers (like me) who really, really, really want to know what's going to happen next which, if you've done your job, is exactly what they should be interested in.

When should you use flashbacks, if at all? Editors and agents see scores of manuscripts with openings slowed to a halt by the weight of flashbacks and explanatory exposition.

Some say to never use them, and that's possible. But there are times a flashback can enrich a story, adding depth and meaning that would otherwise not be there. There are times when, without knowledge of the past, a character's actions will seem unmotivated, and thus not credible.

So when and how do you use flashbacks? I advocate using them only when the knowledge revealed in the flashback is **absolutely critical for understanding what's going on in the story's present**. Beginning writers need to be tough on themselves here. They'll feel like a reader needs to know things about a character that, truthfully, are not necessary for understanding the NOW of the story. It's the NOW that readers want to be immersed in.

Another reason for flashbacks is *necessary characterization*—an example is coming right up.

We pause for notes on how to create a flashback that works.

1. Weave it as seamlessly as possible into the action. Words such as "remembered" and phrases such as "thought of the time when"

are bright red flags that signal to many readers that coming soon to a page near them is a part to skip. Transitions are key.

2. Make the flashback a true scene with action, dialogue, tension, and all the storytelling elements that you use to keep a reader engaged. Avoid *telling* a past event, show it (unless it can be done in one brief, crisp paragraph). Readers want to experience what's happening, not just receive information. A good flashback, for the moment, becomes the "now" of the story.

Here's an example of slipping from the present to the past and back in order to give the reader necessary information about a character. Note: in the story, *lledri* refers to an energy these people can manipulate like magic.

Graeme had been so full of life the day they strolled through Central Park . . . if only she hadn't said, "I thought the Met's new sculpture exhibit was excellent."

Graeme had shrugged. "Perhaps." He gestured at the people who plodded through the park. "But there's little else of excellence from that sorry race."

Ailia's contrary side had reared its head at the unfairness of the bias against the *lessi* that Graeme inherited from his father. "There's plenty of good in them, and you know it."

"I do not." He surveyed the people around them. Dozens wandered, for it was a sunny day. "See their colors, Ailia. Is there kindness or good will anywhere?"

She had looked, and the *lledri* auras around their heads writhed with the nasty burgundy of hostility, the bilious color of lies, the ash-violet of depression, and the bruised red of violence. That, of course, only served to rally her resistance. "Perhaps not here, not now, but there are many good-hearted *lessi*."

He made an exaggerated moue and said, "A wager?"

She picked up the gauntlet. "Yes." She pointed down a curving walk. "I say we'll find a worthy *lessi* that way."

"The stakes?"

She ran her hands over her breasts and down her belly. Oh, that smile of his. He said, "It's a bet."

She congratulated herself on her good luck when they came upon a woman pulling a two-wheeled shopping cart; her aura radiated a rosy gold, the rich hue of caring. Perhaps sixty years old, the woman was stout, anchored to the earth like an oak tree. She stopped before a trio of homeless men who sprawled on ragged blankets.

When she opened a brown paper bag from her cart, Ailia caught the aroma of bologna. The woman took a sandwich from the sack and handed it to one of the men. He sat up and attacked the food.

Graeme spread his arms in surrender, lifted his gaze to the heavens and said, as if to a higher power, "Why have you once again given Ailia victory over your poor servant Graeme?"

She poked him in his ribs and said, "I believe you owe me."

He pulled her into his arms. "I'm ready."

His body let her know that he was indeed ready. Her pulse had quickened, and she had wanted to take him by the hand, find a cluster of bushes, cast a shadow illusion for concealment, and make love. But she had pushed away and said, "If we're so advanced, we should help."

Oh, if only. . .

He had laughed, and then put on a thick French accent. "But of course, *ma cherie.*" Stepping to the woman's side, he gestured to the sack of sandwiches and said, "May I?"

She smiled and nodded, and Graeme took a sandwich from the bag and thrust it at a whiskery man whose bristles made him look like a wild boar.

The boar man scrambled to his feet, digging into a pocket. Too late Ailia saw in his aura the acrid tornado of colors that meant madness. He pulled a knife from a pocket, flicked it open and thrust it into Graeme's chest. Graeme collapsed as if he were a puppet whose strings had been cut.

Ailia had dropped to her knees beside him and plunged *lledri* into his chest to heal the wound with touch—but his heart had been sliced almost in two. There was no way she could mend him. She had looked into his eyes and seen terrible fear . . . and then an even more terrible absence.

If only she hadn't . . .if only. . .

The "if only she hadn't" bookends the flashback to ease you into the past and back to the present. Connective tissue such as this can help move your reader into and out of a flashback and help tie its meaning to the story.

This example, brief at it is (just two manuscript pages), expands the reader's understanding of why the character is depressed and suicidal, yet it has conflict and tension.

Later, to deepen the reader's understanding of the other primary protagonist, this novel uses a mini-flashback to plant the seed for a longer one that added to characterization later. First, the mini-flash:

> Gabe had never found a word for what he saw when people lied. Aura? But it wasn't a glow so much as streaming sparks of translucent, luminescent color that he could "see" even with his eyes closed. He'd never heard of anyone else seeing them. People would probably think it was a good thing, being able to tell when people lied. But he hated it. He'd felt . . . *outside* since he was seven and perceiving the color of lies in action had cost him his best friend.

The character's feeling of not belonging is a powerful motivator for later action, and this brief glimpse needed expanding—but not at this moment in the story. The full history wasn't needed for understanding, but his ability to use *lledri* needed to be introduced and explained, along with planting the seed for a flashback that later expands the experience that motivated his feelings.

His son has inherited his ability, and the effect on the boy resembles autism, which is something the father needs to understand. So, eighty-five pages later, when the other protagonist says to him, "You know the effect that possessing this ability can have on a child, don't you?" this is Gabe's response:

> Oh, yeah, Gabe knew how seeing a weird color in the air can affect a kid. In second grade, he'd seen Marty Simmons swipe an oatmeal cookie from Heather's lunch sack. It was scorched on the bottom like all the cookies Heather's mom made. When Heather noticed Marty eating it, she accused him of taking her cookie.
>
> He had told her his mom had baked cookies yesterday and that Heather was crazy—and a nasty greenish color had flickered around his head. Gabe studied the other kids at the table as they watched Marty tell his lie. Their eyes never shifted and they never reacted to the color swirling around Marty's head, not even when Heather started to cry.

They just couldn't see it. Gabe had decided he wasn't crazy because he knew what he saw was true, but he felt . . . *outside*, as though he was across the room from everybody else. Gabe had wanted to ask his mother about it, but he'd been afraid she would look at him in that scared-angry way that said he was nuts . . . strange . . . weird.

Soon he'd had no friends, and it wasn't until his mother moved and he changed schools that he was able to make himself pretend he was like everybody else and be friendly again.

Both the "mini flash" and the longer flashback were tied directly to the action in the scenes, and the longer one briefly summarizes a scene complete with action and conflict.

My advice: keep flashbacks to a minimum, and avoid, if at all possible, launching into one within the first few pages of your story. A flashback in the wrong place can be a momentum-killer.

word

noun

1 a: something that is said

Section 5: Words

There's a point in the film *Amadeus* where the prince, after hearing one of Mozart's works, comments, "There are too many notes."

In that instance, the man was an ass. However, in my editing practice, I often find too many words. The pace slows. Meaning is muddy. Sentences become clunky. There are words and constructions that I think should be avoided.

Perhaps you've heard the view that you shouldn't use adverbs—bestselling author Elmore Leonard is dead set against them. Mostly, I agree. You should pitilessly weed out many of the adverbs that lurk in your manuscript because they are *telling* posing as *showing*. I'll show you how to avoid those imposters. But don't avoid all adverbs; I'll show you a story-friendly use of "good" adverbs that I've realized.

To help you deliver a crisp, clean narrative, I'll point out:

➤ The bad and the good of adverbs
➤ Weak, wasted, and wrong words
➤ What's wrong with "started to"
➤ Why you should do without "without"
➤ And why you should watch your as.

> "Instead of just theory, your 'rules in action' method gets the message across clearly and concisely."
>
> Nienke Hinton, writer

Words

Adverbs: good? Bad? Yes.

Here's a simple-minded example of one of the reasons adverbs can be the bane of writing for effect. This is fundamental stuff, and I don't mean to insult you…I just want to contrast *effect* to *info*. A story starts with this:

Jimmy walked slowly across the cluttered room.

Simple information. I see, fuzzily, a guy walking. Not very fast (but I can't really picture it). There's stuff in the room (but who knows what).

The effect? Not much. No clear picture comes to mind. First thing to do: ditch the verb/adverb combo and choose a verb that evokes a picture, at the least, and at best characterizes the action. If, for example, your story is suspense, then how about…

Jimmy crept across the cluttered room.

Better. Here are other possibilities, depending on the story:
- ➢ In a fight scene, Jimmy would have *lunged* across the room.
- ➢ If Jimmy is a dancer, then he *glided*.
- ➢ Make Jimmy a burglar and he *skulked*.
- ➢ If Jimmy is in no hurry, then he *ambled*.
- ➢ If Jimmy is in a hurry, then he *dashed*.
- ➢ If Jimmy has been over-served at a bar, then he *weaved*. Or maybe he *tottered*, or *staggered*, or *lurched*, or, my personal favorite, *sloshed*.

Each of those verbs evokes a picture of Jimmy's body moving in specific ways. They are "visual" verbs that created a specific effect in your mind.

Stimulus > response.

There's another bit of lazy writing in the example sentence—the adjective "cluttered." It did nothing to create a picture. At the very least, we should see what the room was cluttered with, e.g.:

Jimmy crept across a room cluttered with shrunken heads.

Ooooo. See how specificity stirs up story questions? Don't you want more? What about the room? Is it dark? Any smells? Sounds? Is anyone else there? What about characterization? Put on Jimmy's skin and…

He was glad that the light of his candle was dim—all those tiny faces staring up at him were entirely too creepy. He set a foot down and winced at a crunch. He froze, listening for sounds of renewed pursuit. But only the scurrying of rats troubled the air, musty with the dust of the dead.

Rats?

Oh, fine.

Let's get back to adverbs. There's a reason adverbs rob you of effect.

Adverbs are *telling*

I believe that adverbs that modify action verbs are merely a form of *telling*. They are abstractions of action, pallid substitutes for the real thing, mere stand-ins. As a result, they rarely give the reader much of an experience. For example, one of my clients wrote,

She grinned mischievously.

Now, the average reader would take that in, plug in some sort of vague image, keep on rolling and never realize she had been cheated—but she was. There's a much more lively and concrete picture to be created in the reader's mind. For example:

She grinned, mischief sparking in her eyes.

In the original, because you have to interpret "mischievously" (what, exactly, is that?) the effect is to evoke an unsure image of a grin. In the second, you see a face in action: lips curve, you see a grin, you see eyes, you see playful activity behind those eyes. All that from four extra words chosen for effect. Or, hey, what about something like this…

> She grinned like a fox that had just found the keys to the henhouse.

The third example goes beyond word choice to tap into meaning and characterization beyond a simple visual.

Watch out for adverbs in dialogue tags

Many writers use adverbs to explain dialogue rather than show how the dialogue is delivered. For example:

> "This is my dialogue," he said hesitantly.

That's lazy use of an adverb. You could say something like. . .

> He hesitated, then said, "This is my dialogue."

But that's not precisely what "said hesitantly" means, is it? There would be a hesitation in there somewhere. Wouldn't it be more effective if we *dramatized* the hesitation so the reader experienced it rather than read about it? For instance, let's *show* it this way:

> "This. . ." He swallowed and glanced at her face. ". . . is my dialogue."

Go on an adverb hunt and replace them with the action they only hint at and you'll be writing for effect.

But not all adverbs are bad guys

I was reviewing one of my manuscripts the other day and spotted, gasp, an adverb. Here's the sentence:

> She saw Murphy, like a big, round boulder parting a stream of girly secretaries cramming in a buzz of noontime shopping—except this boulder stared blatantly at their bobbing chests as they passed.

"Stared blatantly?" Damn. Another case of making an adverb try to do the work of real description. To be fair, this was from my first novel, written several years ago, on the lower slopes of my learning curve.

In this case the answer lay, as usual, in the verb. I swapped out "stared blatantly" for "leered." Much better, giving a clear picture with fewer words. While I was at it, I tightened the sentence a little, too:

> She saw Murphy, like a big, round boulder parting a stream of girly secretaries cramming in a buzz of noontime shopping, leering at their bobbing chests.

And then I came upon a pair of adverbs in one sentence…

> He found Emmaline to be annoyingly cheerful but pleasingly proficient.

But these adverbs worked for me. Wait, I thought, how come they seem right when I've preached loud and long to avoid adverbs? Then I noticed that these modified *adjectives* rather than *verbs*.

Good cholesterol and bad cholesterol?

There was a time when we believed that all cholesterol was bad. Then we learned that there is good cholesterol and bad cholesterol.

Well, I changed my position that all adverbs are suspect, if not bad. I think there are "good" adverbs, the ones that add just the right flavor to an adjective, enhancing it with a more complete shade of meaning.

Consider the sentence describing Emmaline. Could I have achieved what I wanted, which was to give insight into one character's feeling and attitudes toward another, without the adverbs?

> He found Emmaline to be cheerful but proficient.

Nope. I've lost how the viewpoint character feels about Emmaline's personality.

I went on a search for other adverbs (using Microsoft Word's Find tool to locate "ly" in words).

> Her fair cheeks fetchingly reddened by the cold, she looked no older than a teenager.

Yep, for me this works as well. It would have been okay to write. . .

> Her fair cheeks reddened by the cold, she looked no older
> than a teenager.

. . .and you would have gotten a picture. But take "fetchingly" out and you lose the point-of-view character's reaction to the girl's cheeks. With the addition of the adverb to this adjective, you also get the character's *experience*, i.e. his emotional reaction to the appearance he sees—fetching, attractive.

The pattern I was discovering seemed to be that adverbs are a positive addition when coupled to adjectives in order to add a point-of-view character's nuance to what would otherwise be simple description. Another instance from the same manuscript:

> He loved the Staffordshire blue-and-white rose pattern,
> beautifully detailed and botanically accurate right down to
> the thorns on the stems.

Take "beautifully" and "botanically" out of that sentence and I think it loses both meaning and flavor. Once more:

> She changed her disguise to the queenly dignity of a white-
> haired society matron she'd met in Brussels.

Now, to "show" without the adverb would have required something like this:

> She changed her disguise to that of a dignified, white-haired
> society matron with the manner of a queen, whom she'd met
> in Brussels.

Not as effective, is it?

Here's an example taken from a client's manuscript of a good adverb and bad adverb in the same sentence:

> A young waiter with carefully streaked hair smiled sugges-
> tively at her.

For me, the first adverb expands the picture of the waiter's hair by giving a hint of precision in the arrangement of the streaks, which tells me something about him as well. But I'd like to see the second adverb replaced with something more truly pictorial.

When you go hunting for adverbs, it's when they modify action that you should consider looking for a better verb to do the job, and when they amplify adjectives that you may find adverbs to be good cholesterol.

"I have read a lot about the craft of writing, but in my experience, no one has ever suggested the possibility of 'good' and 'bad' adverbs before. Thank you."

Lisa Miles, writer

> "Most of what we get should never have left the writer's hand."
>
> An acquisitions editor

Words

Weed out weak, wasted & wrong words

It's a cliché, it's a truth: Every word counts. Reading and imagining and experiencing your narrative is a cumulative process. Meanings and usage add up, bit by bit, into gestalts that insert what's happening to the character into your reader's mind.

Weak words fail to deliver vivid pictures and actions—do you want that? Waste words take up space and slow the pace—and are among the first discouraging things a professional spots. Even worse, wrong words, words used in an incorrect way, confuse your reader and take them out of the story, not to mention costing you credibility and suspension of belief. Yet the manuscripts of novice writers are filled with just that. Here are some of the worst offenders.

-ing

Let's start with half a word. "Inging," over-use of the present participle, frequently slows pace and mushes meaning. More often than not, "ings" should be "eds" for crisp writing.

> She was polishing her glasses as she searched for the right words.

I think this is passive and slow to create a picture in the reader's mind. Much more to the point, and quicker to create a picture, is:

She polished her glasses as she searched for the right words.

Examples from samples I've received:

The rain was turning into snow as they drove. *(turned)*

Dylan was circling the cabin. *(circled)*

Joanne was hoping that she would get to see her family skiing. *(hoped, ski)*

Bob was getting more and more nervous. *(grew)*

"No," the heavy woman said, rummaging through the shopping bag she was carrying. *(carried)*

Lulu was feeling tipsy. *(felt)*

There are times, though, when "ing" (for me) helps convey an ongoing process. For example, consider "Thinking of his face, she hesitated." versus "She thought of his face and hesitated." For me the first version puts a thoughtful look on the character's face and creates a pause in whatever she's doing, and the second version is just action.

some

A waste word, a verbal habit something like the "uh" many people use in speech. A few examples (I almost said "some," but that was so vague); see how cutting the "somes" costs nothing yet makes the sentence crisper.

Married women always wore ~~some~~ bangles around both their wrists.

Do you have ~~some~~ pressing business?

My big band attained ~~some~~ modest local fame and national press.

There was ~~some~~ movement as the crocodiles attempted to steer clear.

She had ~~some~~ packing to do.

~~Some~~ tantalizing smells were wafting towards them from across the river. *(and let's change were wafting to wafted)*

He had to have ~~some~~ new tires installed.

very

Another waste word.

William was one of ~~very~~ *(the)* few who knew. *(not needed)*

I want the ~~very~~ best students. *(redundant—best is best)*

Mr. Simpson has been ~~very~~ eager to meet you. *(there are no degrees of eagerness—redundant)*

. . .in the ~~very~~ coldest part of winter. *(redundant—coldest is coldest)*

They were ~~very~~ hungry. *(starving or famished are more specific, more effective)*

During lunch she becomes ~~very~~ quiet. *(redundant—quiet is quiet)*

of

In my first novel a reader picked up on a habit I had of overusing "of" as in, "He emptied his pot of coffee." I used my word processor's search tool to hunt for "of" and found many that I could change to either a possessive or use an adjective, e.g., "He emptied his coffee pot." This may seem mindlessly simple to you, but I found lots of places to tighten my narrative, which helped with pace and clarity.

eyes

This is an example of improper usage. Many writers use "eyes" when what they really mean is gaze, or glance, or stare. Some examples in which I take the usage to the next logical step:

Her eyes were on the floor. *(Luckily, no one stepped on them.)*

His blue eyes bored into her. (*And then blood gushed from the two holes in her belly.*)

She felt the woman's eyes searching for her. (*It tickled when they slid across her face.*)

His tired eyes land on me as he glances around the room. (*Then they drop to the floor and roll under the couch.*)

My eyes follow the headlights. (*I ignore the wrenching pain when they leave their sockets.*)

Roger kept his eyes on the road. (*He realized his mistake when the ice cream truck ran over them.*)

Fire up your word processor, open your manuscript, launch the search tool, and type these weak, wasted, or wrong words in the *Find what:* box and go hunting for opportunities to make your narrative stronger and sharper.

Words

Don't get me started

A common locution that I see in manuscripts (and published novels) is "started to." Also, "began to." While there are times when those expressions are appropriate, they aren't nearly as frequent as some writers seem to feel.

When/if you use "started to" and "began to" in your narrative, spend a moment and think about what the words really mean. Another usage that tangles meaning is "with." I'll get to that later.

Here are some examples of "started to" drawn from a number of submissions.

> When we started to get repeat responses to stimuli, we changed the system.

This says that the two things happened simultaneously, although they couldn't have; they didn't change the system until after the repeat responses occurred. Rewrite:

> After we got repeat responses to the stimuli, we changed the system.

What about this one?

> She turned away and started to laugh.

What is the start of a laugh? "H—" and then silence? No, in this narrative, the character laughed. Rewrite:

She turned away and laughed.

Tears make an appearance:

Her tears started to flow.

So they appeared in the corners of her eyes and then just sat there? Nope, if they flowed at all, they rolled on down her cheeks. Rewrite:

Her tears flowed.

Getting a character moving:

Larry slid from his stool and started to follow the beggar.

So did Larry get his feet on the floor, lift a foot, and then stop? Take a step or two and stop? No, he followed the beggar. See how much crisper it is to say:

Larry slid from his stool and followed the beggar.

Can an action be partial?

He started to laugh but stopped short when he saw how angry she was.

Another "H—" here? Wouldn't this create a better picture of what might really happen?

He laughed, but then stopped when he saw her anger.

What about thoughts?

His mind started to whirl with crazy ideas.

So what's the idea here? His mind starts, like a song beginning, and then, "r-r-r-r," dies out? Not likely.

His mind whirled with crazy ideas.

Be careful of continuity.

> She started to sob and Steve held the weeping child in his arms.

Okay, if she only starts (which can mean that she stops), then how come she's weeping when she gets into Steve's embrace? Rewrite:

> She sobbed, and Steve held the weeping child in his arms.

Actually, written this way, "weeping" isn't needed.

> She sobbed and Steve held the child in his arms.

A confusing mix of actions:

> She began to back away when a faint movement in the yard stopped her.

A really confusing set of words for me. She was backing and a movement stopped her? Doesn't seem possible. Rewrite:

> She backed away, but then stopped at the sight of movement in the yard.

Sometimes, though, "started" is right.

> She stopped him when he started to rise to his feet.

This one is okay because the action was interrupted.

Do without the "with" redux

In the Dialogue section I bemoaned saying things with "with," but there's another way in which "with" can befuddle your narrative—when it adds things together nonsensically. When you think about what the words really mean, there are times when "with" is the wrong word—and it's your job to think about what words really mean.

He watched her with a satisfied smile.

So his teeth are capable of vision? Maybe, in a sci-fi adventure, but most of us use our eyes for this sort of thing. Also, this is *telling*—what does a "satisfied smile" *look* like? Rewrite:

He watched her and smiled, satisfied.

This one has one heck of a dog.

The dog started to chase the sheep with a snarl.

A double whammy: first the "started to," and then how did the dog hold the snarl with which he chased the sheep? In his teeth? How does one use a snarl in a chase, anyway? Rewrite:

The dog snarled and then chased the sheep.

Misuse of roaring.

With a roar of encouragement, the watchers pushed him back into the fight.

So how did they get a grip on the roar in order to push with it? Aren't those things slippery? Rewrite:

The watchers roared encouragement and pushed him back into the fight.

A tragic use of "with."

She ran into his arms with a strangled sob.

Where did she get the strangled sob? Who strangled the poor thing?

On the other hand, sometimes I could use one of these.

Margaret straightened her back with a groan.

I never thought to use a groan to straighten my back. Rewrite:

Margaret groaned when she straightened her back.

A touching use of "with."

He touched it with a worried expression.

So did he place his face against it? Rewrite:

He touched it, his worry shown by his expression.

Do a search for "started to" and "began to" and "with" and see if you find any of these potential befuddlements lurking in your narrative.

~~without~~

Do without "without"

I'll wager you've seen one or more of these phrases in stories:

> ➢ Without a sound

> ➢ Without a glance

> ➢ Without a doubt

> ➢ Without a thought

> ➢ Without a word

You might have even used them.

It seems to me that most of the time these phrases are about as useful as your appendix. They are comfortable-feeling collections of words that describe a negative, an absence. But I think they are frequently lazy writing. They are a missed opportunity to write for effect.

If whatever it is the story is doing without isn't there, why bring it up? You, the writer, control absolutely everything the character and the reader experience. If you don't put something into the narrative, it doesn't exist, does it? So why tell the reader that what isn't there isn't there? Actually, in most cases the writer intends meaning, it's just that using "without" can leave the reader missing the intended sense of what's happening.

Here are some examples, including a few that come from samples I've received.

Without a sound

He crossed the room without a sound.

You, the author, control what the reader "hears." If you don't supply a sound, there is none. In my view, here "without a sound" is redundant. Do you hear anything if the narrative says this?

He crossed the room.

Nope. In this case the author probably wanted to indicate the stealthy nature of his movement. If so, don't do it with an absence, do it with intent.

Stepping lightly to make no sound, he crossed the room.

Or why not show rather than tell? For example:

He removed his shoes and tiptoed across the room in his socks.

Don't you automatically imagine his movement as being silent?

Without a glance

She picked up her bag and walked off without a backward glance.

Okay, this hints at something going on in the character, but only hints. Wouldn't it be better, from a characterization point of view, to do something such as:

She picked up her bag and walked off, resisting the urge to look back, to see his face one more time.

Without a thought

She made her decision without a second thought.

Sure, you'll tell me that the writer is trying to characterize here, that perhaps the character is impulsive. But why do it with an absence? Could it be more positively stated? For example:

> She plunged ahead and made her decision.

Without a word

> Alex stepped into the room without a word.

So he left it outside the room? Will he have go back and get it if he needs it? Which word? Rather than raise all these questions in the minds of astute readers, why not just:

> Alex stepped into the room.

Here's another "without a word":

> "Let's go," she breathed, excited and a little frightened. Without a word, they turned as one to go.

I think it's the "without a word" phrase that seems least likely to contribute. If you, the writer, don't put any words on the page for the character to say, then they weren't said.

I can see, perhaps, a need to characterize an action. I think the following attempts to do that:

> Jessica scooped the mug up and marched off without a word.

But it could do more if it were something like:

> Jessica bit back a retort, scooped up the mug, and marched off.

There are times "without" is useful, of course. From a sample:

> She felt a twinge of regret that she would be leaving Loren without a word of goodbye.

BTW, I try to avoid using "felt." I think the above would be stronger if it were:

> She regretted that she would be leaving Loren without a word of goodbye.

To be fair about this, I searched my own work for "without a." I found these in the first novel:

> She hung up without a goodbye, which suited him fine.

This seems to work because the absence of expected behavior is what the character notices.

> He sagged and left without a look back.

Here the "without a look back" got cut.

In novel number two I found a "without a glance back." I think it should be removed, although I was tempted. . .
I also found two uses of "without a word" that I immediately cut.

The third novel:

> Then Dudley said, without an ounce of his usual sarcasm, "I'm sure it is, pardner."

Seems to me the phrase works here to characterize the speech. If I took it out, you wouldn't get the tone, and it is the absence of sarcasm that counts. I think the construction also suggests that the recipient of this speech (the POV character) expects sarcasm from Dudley.

I think that there are times when the absence of something can be meaningful. In the following example, someone is running a horse (Dusty) through a pasture.

> Ten feet from the gully's edge, without a hint of warning, Dusty turned at a right angle and raced away from the trench.

Ordinarily, a horse's behavior sends signals to the rider, especially about a significant change in direction. Mentioning the absence here lets us know that what happens next is totally unexpected.

Jesse left the saddle and flew straight ahead, riding air.

Or how about this:

A cigarette without a light is as useless as a kiss without a pucker.

When I searched novel number four, I found no instances of "without a." Good for me.

This writing thing is a learning curve that all of us climb, phrase by phrase. But it's interesting, isn't it?

Words

Watch your as

As I sipped my coffee this morning, I typed, "Watch your as."

What's wrong with that bit of narrative? Well, I'm not about to be able to sip my coffee and type simultaneously unless I've got three hands. Oh, I guess it's possible—if I were sipping my coffee through a straw while typing. But who does that?

We're about to pick at a nit here—the misuse of the "as" construction in narratives.

I suspect you've seen a phrase such as the example above, and it may not have struck you that something was awry. When you examine it, though, it describes a highly improbable event.

Y'see, in this situation "as" means simultaneously. Often I see writers use "as" when they should be using "when," or sometimes "after."

In the opening example, it should be something like:

I sipped my coffee, and then I typed, "Watch your as."

Following are examples collected from samples and manuscripts I've received.

Morgan collapsed onto the sofa as his knees gave way.

To my mind, the collapse was the *result* of his knees giving way. He wouldn't collapse as they gave way because they haven't finished giving way, and so are not "collapsible." The fix here is to use "when" (after would also work):

> Morgan collapsed onto the sofa when his knees gave way.

What about this one?

> As I flipped the switch the kitchen was flooded with light and I saw Portia on the floor.

You see it coming, don't you? While I'm at it, I'll get rid of a "was."

> When I flipped the light switch, light flooded the kitchen and I saw Portia on the floor.

That was a clear case of "when" because light would not flood the kitchen until after the switch was flipped. With "as," the switch could be anywhere in the process of completing the circuit, including before it's completed.

"As" often ignores a stimulus and response scenario.

> George stiffened as the man swore a solemn oath.

I see the stiffening as a reaction to the nature (and content) of the oath, not the act of swearing. How would George know it was solemn until it was spoken? An adjustment:

> The man swore a solemn oath. George stiffened.

Some uses of "as" are downright sloppy:

> Lee jokes as he swigs from his bottle.

Have you ever tried telling a joke while simultaneously taking a swig from a bottle? If that's your habit, remind me not to buy you a drink. How it might be written:

> Lee swigs from his bottle and then jokes.

From a romance:

> As their eyes met her knees turned to butter.

Nope, the buttery knees were a reaction to the meeting of their gazes (not eyes). "When" tells you the sequence of events.

> When their gazes met, her knees turned to butter.

From horror:

> Chills ran down Tim's spine as he realized that evil was close
> to his son.

Once again, there's a cause-and-effect time sequence necessary here, to my way of thinking. Doesn't it seem logical that the chills are caused by the realization, and thus can't be running anywhere until after the realization?

> When Tim realized that evil was close to his son, chills ran
> down his spine.

Side note: I would suggest to the writer that "ran down his spine" is hackneyed, if not clichéd, and to look for a fresh way to describe the reaction.
Here's one from an accomplished writer:

> Instinct saved my face from being slashed as I ducked away
> at the last second.

Once again, we're dealing with a linear cause and effect. Seems to me that his instincts caused the ducking, and therefore had to precede it. The instinctive motivation to move and the movement itself can't be simultaneous. Here's one way to do it with a semi-colon:

> Instinct saved my face from being slashed; I ducked away at
> the last second.

Another cause-and-effect situation:

> Squirrels scattered as my bike tires hit the cinder alley behind
> our house.

Again, "when" seems to me to be the more accurate word. The squirrels react to the sound of the tires hitting the gravel, which can only be generated when they hit, and *then* the squirrels hear it.

An ambivalent usage:

He quivered as her feminine odor wafted into his nostrils.

This one is borderline. He could certainly do the quivering as the odor wafted in, but the writer's clear intent was to let the reader know that the odor caused the quiver. I think it would have created a more logical sense of what was happening with:

He quivered when her feminine odor wafted into his nostrils.

There are, of course, times when the "as" construction serves a narrative well by describing things that can, and should, happen simultaneously. For example,

Marcie laughed as she swung Amy back and forth.

As he lathered his face, he debated whether to wear a suit or not.

She gnawed her lip in frustration as she watched him leave.

Hmm. As I look at these four examples, I find myself thinking that maybe "while" would serve better than "as" in some of them.

I suggest (and I've done this with my own work) doing a search for "as" (remember to select "Find whole words only" or it'll drive you crazy) and see if your usage truly makes sense. Or if perhaps "while" is a better alternative, or what you really need is a "when" or an "after."

Section 6: Workouts
Your all-important first 16 lines

Agents and editors report that they look for reasons to reject, and that they can usually make that decision based on the first page, or perhaps two. With good reason, too—after reading hundreds of submissions, these pros are attuned to distinct clues as to:

➢ The quality of writing that they will encounter throughout the manuscript
➢ The appeal of the voice
➢ Tension in the story

In a properly formatted novel manuscript—double-spaced, one-inch margins, 12-point type—chapters begin about a third of the way down the page. Generally, that translates into approximately sixteen lines of narrative.

Those sixteen lines can be make-or-break with an agent or acquisitions editor. You need to make it virtually impossible for them to resist turning the page.

You must *compel* them to turn the page.

On my blog, *Flogging the Quill*, I do a critique called the "Flogometer." Writers send me their first chapter or prologue, and I challenge them to compel me to turn the page. Then I critique the sample for its strengths and shortcomings, doing some edits and making suggestions.

"Interests me" isn't good enough, and it can't be good enough for you. Your first sixteen lines have to have the power to *force* a page turn. If they don't, your book risks being tossed.

Following are opening pages from novels sent to me by people working hard at becoming published. I'll give you the opening in double-spaced manuscript form so there's plenty of space for you to make notes, including line edits that you feel are needed, and comments or direction you would give the writer about what works and what doesn't.

> "No one else I've read seems to get the redundancies and non-story snippets out of the text like you do."
>
> Clayton Lindemuth, writer

After you exercise your critical faculties, I'll give you the critique I did for the Flogometer. Once you've finished this book, pull out the first sixteen lines of your novel and think about how well they meet the challenge.

One more thing: this is, perhaps, the most severe of tests in that I don't consider titles or blurbs or query letters or whatever else would ordinarily accompany the narrative. On the other hand, as Miss Snark, the literary agent/blogger said, "It's the story that counts."

No, really, do the work

If you're like me, you'll be tempted to just read the samples and then go on to the critiques. Trust me, that's not a good idea. I guarantee nothing will focus you on the merits and shortcomings of writing (including your own) like having a pencil in hand and the duty to edit.

I strongly urge you to strike through things you'd cut, add things you'd add, indicate where you might move pieces of narrative, and write in comments that help the writer. You'll find yourself applying the lessons from this book and seeing a narrative in new ways—and that can lead to you seeing your own writing with far fresher eyes.

Answer the tough questions. Is it compelling? Does it hook you? Does the writing create an experience in your mind?

One of the things you'll learn from your work is the subjectivity of editing. You may find yourself with views that oppose mine.

But I think you'll also find plenty of agreement. Best of all, you'll begin to apply a critical eye to narrative, which can lead to clearer vision when you look at your own work.

Keep in mind the six elements of a good story:
- ➤ Tension
- ➤ Story questions
- ➤ Voice
- ➤ Clarity
- ➤ Scene setting
- ➤ Character

Conventions I'll use to show editing:
- ➤ Deletions are shown with ~~strikethrough~~.
- ➤ Additions are **bold**.
- ➤ Comments are in parentheses and *(italicized)*.
- ➤ Phrases to think about are <u>underlined</u>.

One other thing: this section will also give you a clear idea of how I edit. With me, it's more of a partnership, as I'm sure it is with many other editors. You don't invest as much of yourself as good editing takes without caring, or without lending as much of a hand as you can.

Cave editor.

Workout 1

Jan, a writer in Australia, sent these first sixteen lines (thus the Brit punctuation). This is the sample you encountered in the Benchmark chapter in the beginning of this book. Think back to what you thought then. Will you see it differently now?

'Michael's gone!' Julia screamed into the payphone outside Flinders Street Train Station.

'Calm down, Mrs Stewart. She'll be with you shortly.'

Julia bristled at the matter-of-factness of the receptionist's voice. 'I don't care if she's with the Queen. My husband is missing. I think I'm losing my mind.'

'Please hold and I'll see if I can interrupt.'

Click. Mozart replaced the receptionist's voice. The familiar hold music from the past sounded surreal against the background tram and traffic noise of the Melbourne thoroughfare.

A pedestrian bumped into her daughter's stroller, turning Shellie to tears.

'Stop that, you bad girl!' Julia rolled the stroller under the phone box, putting her child out of the way of the Friday afternoon commuters.

Shellie reached out and cried louder.

'Arrgghh!' Julia dropped the receiver, picked up the three year old and settled her on her hip. Shellie quieted, distracted now by an earring.

Ignoring her, Julia reached for the dangling receiver, and found silence. 'Hello? Hello!' *Don't be gone. I don't have any more change.*

'I thought I'd lost you.' The receptionist's cheerfulness was enough to piss off anyone.

Would you turn the page? Mark up the sample with cuts, ideas, whatever you'd advise this writer to do to improve this narrative.

I wanted to see what was next

Good story questions, good writing, a likeable voice—all contributed to my turning the page. I like starting with a scene, and the very first line introduces an element of tension. However, I have thoughts for improvement.
My notes:

'Michael's gone!' Julia screamed into the payphone ~~outside Flinders Street Train Station~~. *(If you want the reader to get that 'Michael's gone!' is screamed, then you need to clue the reader first, i.e.* Julia screamed, 'Michael's gone!' into the payphone. *I felt that naming the train station felt like an authorial intrusion here. I'd leave it at the pay phone and mention the train station later.)*

'Calm down, Mrs Stewart. She'll be with you shortly.'

Julia bristled at the matter-of-factness of the receptionist's voice. 'I don't care if she's with the Queen. My husband is missing. I think I'm losing my mind.' *(While this seems okay, I wonder if it's enough. As it turns out, her husband has been missing for two hours, and she's pretty much panicked. "Bristle" seems too mild to be consistent with panic. A thought-starter: what about an internal rhetorical question, something like:* How could the damned receptionist be so matter-of-fact? 'I don't care if she's…*)*

'Please hold and I'll see if I can interrupt.'

~~Click.~~ Mozart replaced the receptionist's voice. The ~~familiar hold~~ music ~~from the past~~ sounded surreal against the background tram **noise outside Flinders Street Train Station** and the traffic ~~noise~~ of the Melbourne thoroughfare. *(The reference to "from the past" confused me, and it seemed to place more significance on the music than I think is necessary. As you see, here's where I'd work in the train station.)*

A pedestrian bumped into her daughter's stroller, turning Shellie to tears.

'Stop that, you bad girl!' Julia rolled the stroller under the phone box, putting her child out of the way of ~~the~~ Friday afternoon commuters.

Shellie ~~reached out and~~ cried louder.

'Arrgghh!' Julia dropped the receiver, picked up the three-year-old and settled her on her hip. Shellie quieted, distracted now by an earring. *(The "distracted" part is telling where this could be shown. For example:* Shellie toyed with an earring and quieted.*)*

Ignoring her, Julia reached for the dangling receiver and found silence. 'Hello? Hello!' *Don't be gone. I don't have any more change.*

'I thought I'd lost you.' The receptionist's cheerfulness was enough to piss off anyone. *(While I agree that the tone might piss anyone off, I don't think that a woman in a state of panic would be thinking of that in this way. Thoughtstarter: what about something like "Julia wanted to scream at the cheery voice, but choked it back." as a way to show her emotions and frame of mind?)*

> Nice work from Jan. I advised her to keep at it, focus on finding ways to show us, and to keep the protagonist's emotional state firmly in mind when she describes reactions, etc.

Workout 2

The first sixteen lines of Irene's YA paranormal novel:

A Gnome Takes A Club To My Knuckles

Until I lived at Helping Hand, my life was pretty normal. There was school, baseball games, friends, and the usual stuff. The plantation changed it all.

Angel, one of my friends there, said that the plantation was on the between. *Things crossed over like in the Bermuda Triangle. Sometimes—as with the disappearance of Buddy Knoll—the between just sucked someone or something into itself as if it was hungry.*

Mick Grady

My name's Michael Grady, but my friends call me Mick. I'm fourteen. Aunt Liza brought me to The Helping Hand Plantation on a Thursday afternoon in early June. Helping Hand is a temporary place for children who have a family, but their family can't take care of them for a while. Aunt Liza had lost her job, so I had to live there until she got back on her feet.

I was assigned to the North Swamp Dorm and my dorm mother, Ms. Porter, led me up a winding staircase and down a long hallway.

"All the children, except for Tate Thunder, are on a field trip to New Orleans today," she said, her shoes tapping a beat on the hardwood floor. "Tate hurt his leg playing basketball, so he's around somewhere." She stopped outside a door. "You're in here."

I stepped in and Ms. Porter disappeared down the hall. There were six twin beds, separated by a nightstand—three were on the right wall, three on the left. I spotted my luggage (snip)

Mark up the narrative above and decide if you'd have turned the page.

No go for me.

I'm sure many will disagree (remember how subjective this is), but I wasn't compelled to turn the page. What, you might ask, stopped me, considering that enticing tidbit at the top about a kid's disappearance and *the between*? And what about the gnome?

Because that was the only really interesting stuff on the page. After the narrator told me (didn't show me) some information, we got into an entirely mundane arrival of a boy at a temporary housing site. Yes, he has difficulties, what with his Aunt Liza and all, but there doesn't seem to be much jeopardy attached.

I guess that, for me, this lacked the promise of a well-told story. First was the authorial intrusion to tell me things about this place that, I think, would have better been discovered. Second was the lack of tension in what followed.

It's not that this writer can't do that. In fact, she did, just a sentence or two beyond her opening page. Cutting and rearranging just a little, here's what she had. Imagine the manuscript starting with this:

There were six twin beds, separated by nightstands—three on the right wall, three on the left. I spotted my luggage on the right middle bed. Fear crawled inside me and—just for a minute—I pictured myself stuck in this place until I turned eighteen.

"No," I said. Hot tears teased the corners of my eyes.

I sat on the bed next to my luggage. That's when a tiny man jumped on the bed and beat on my hand with a small, wooden club.

Now, this was just six lines of narrative, and I'm a whole lot more hooked than I was by the original sixteen. All that stuff about where he is and why he's there can be handled by slipping it in with bits and pieces as this interesting scene develops.

Look at all the story questions raised in these six lines:
- ➤ Where is the boy?
- ➤ Why is he there?
- ➤ How could he be stuck there?
- ➤ Why does it make him cry?
- ➤ And what's with the tiny man whacking him on the hand?

This narrative even lets you know that the narrator is a boy under eighteen without telling us so. The only area needing improvement is the reference to "tiny" and "small wooden club." Tiny could be better defined — just how tiny is he? And what's "small" in the context of a "tiny" man? For example, what about *showing* us rather than *telling* us with something like:

That's when a tiny man no taller than a coffeepot jumped on the bed and beat on my

hand with a wooden club the size of a teaspoon.

My advice to Irene was to skip all the explanations and get to the STORY. Find a way, with dialogue and internal monologue, to weave the rest in.

Workout 3

Patricia Bates sent her opening to *Flogging the Quill* for a critique, and a few months later she wrote this to me:

> I just wanted to drop you a line and say thank you for the flog you did for me some time ago. I took your advice and reworked the lines, the style a bit and now I am sitting on a contract with Champagne Books to publish *The Master's Mistress*.

Later, when I asked for permission to use the critique in this book, she asked her new agent if it was okay. After reviewing my critique, her agent, Ellen, said yes and added this:

> He was spot on with his editorial comments! Did I mention that I hate the over use of flashbacks too?

See what you think.

Pat's first sixteen lines:

Amoda Ni Cormac tossed three more logs onto the flames before turning to grab the large pot of water to boil. She tensed as she heard heavy footsteps approach. A shudder raced through her and she set the pot down softly.

Amoda gathered her skirts in her hand and tiptoed over to the distant corner of the kitchen. Moving aside the wooden door, she slipped inside the tight crawlspace. She ran her hands over her the goose-prickled flesh of her bare arms and winced as she encountered the bruises from her last beating. She cringed as memories flooded through her. Once more she relived the violence that invaded her nights.

His heavy weight on her chest made her struggles futile. Amoda bucked and twisted under him, finally freeing her hands. She scratched at his face, raking her nails deeply across the weathered skin, drawing blood and curses of pain. All she wanted was to be left alone.

The stench of stale wine and tobacco filled her senses, drowning her in a sense of helplessness, of desperation and added to her horror. She screamed, her fists pummeling his shoulders, her fingers pulling at his hair, her legs kicking out at him harder as she felt the calloused hand creeping under her tunic, mauling a bare breast.

"Too much for the Prince to handle, I say. What he doesn't know can't trouble him."

What do you think? Turn the page? Any edits needed?

The immediate flashback discouraged me

There is good writing here, and a well-imagined world. I would much rather be plunged into it rather than reliving it. As I've said before, the reader wants to know what's happening now, not then. By the way, the "beating" turns out to be more of a rape, so I wondered why it was called a beating. I believe that, while the writer is working hard to introduce a sympathetic character to us, we're being told something the writer thinks we need to know. Why not start with the beating/rape as a live scene rather than history?

My notes:

Amoda Ni Cormac tossed three more logs onto the flames before turning to grab the large pot of water to boil. She tensed ~~as~~ **when** she heard ~~heavy~~ footsteps approach. A shudder raced through her and she set the pot down softly. *(A few nit-picks: "large" is a vague and relative conclusion word, and doesn't actually contribute to a picture. If you want to show that it's large, you could use another way to let the reader understand that. For example, it would be heavy, right? What about:* Amoda Ni Cormac tossed three more logs onto the flames, and then strained to lift the pot of water to boil. *Using adverbs such as "softly" aren't truly descriptive most of the time. I try to avoid them. For example, here she could ease the pot back down, which shows rather than tells. I changed "as" to "when" because she did not tense simultaneously with hearing the footsteps—the sound has to come first.)*

Amoda gathered her skirts ~~in her hand~~ and tiptoed ~~over~~ to the distant corner of the kitchen. Moving aside the wooden door, she slipped inside the tight crawlspace. She ran her hands over her the goose-prickled flesh of her ~~bare~~ arms and winced ~~as~~ **when** she encountered ~~the~~ bruises from her last beating. She cringed as memories flooded through her. Once more she relived the violence that invaded her nights. *(Argh! So we go to a flashback. I wouldn't here. Other things: in my understanding, and in houses today, a crawlspace is beneath the floor of the building. So I don't understand her getting into one here. There are bits of overwriting. For example, when a* *woman gathers her skirts, by necessity she uses her hands, so adding that bit of detail is just clutter because a reader will automatically imagine the process. In this case, "distant" is also a vague and relative descriptor—it doesn't actually help give a picture of the room. Furthermore, is it actually needed? What does it matter how far away the corner is as long as she hides?)*

His heavy weight on her chest made her struggles futile. Amoda bucked and twisted under him, finally freeing her hands. She scratched ~~at~~ his face, raking her nails deeply across the weathered skin, drawing blood and curses of pain. All she wanted was to be left alone.

*The stench of stale wine and tobacco filled her senses, drowning her in a sense of helplessness, of desperation and added to her horror. She screamed, ~~her fists~~ **and pummeled** ~~pummeling~~ his shoulders.~~, her fingers pulling at~~ **She pulled his hair** ~~, her legs kicking out~~ **and kicked** ~~at~~ him ~~harder as~~ **when** ~~she felt the~~ **his** calloused hand ~~creeping~~ **crept** under her tunic, ~~mauling a bare~~ **and mauled her** breast. (Too many "ings" here. And you gave the action to parts of her body rather than her. This is a scene of violent action, and I think that short, active sentences do a better job of delivering the experience. "ing" words are softer, and lack the bite and punch of the past tense I substituted. Another thought—since this is a rape, wouldn't he shove his hand under his tunic rather than creep it? IMO.)*

"Too much for the Prince to handle, I say. What he doesn't know can't trouble him."
(Could use a dialogue tag here to show who says this.)

The rest of the pages were similar, with good writing slowed down here and there by bits of overwriting. There was more backstory, which further slowed getting me involved with this girl's story. I suggested Pat look further down the narrative line for a better, more immediate place to start the story.

I liked the work, and encouraged Pat to keep at it. I suggested that she look for ways to tighten the narrative, make it crisp and active. And I told her to, above all, get into what's happening now and avoid the past until she had us hooked. Apparently her subsequent hard work paid off.

Workout 4

The first sixteen lines of Rob's YA fantasy:

In the kitchen, the kettle was blowing its top like a runaway steam train.

Eliza wrapped a towel around the handle and heaved it from the stove. Wispy curls of steam rose to the ceiling as she poured the boiling water into the waiting teapot, infusing the air with the delicate scent of bergamot.

She left the tea to brew for a moment when something caught her eye, and she automatically looked up. Did something just pass by the window? Wiping the condensation from the glass, she peered out past the garden to the dark tangled trees of Bracken Wood beyond.

Eventually, she shook her head, convincing herself that it was nothing, and poured the Earl Grey into a fine china cup.

A radio babbled away in the background, but its half-heard gossip was more a distraction than anything else and she reached over to switch it off. She raised the cup absently to her mouth to take a sip but ended up scalding her lips. With a wince, she placed the cup back on the kitchen table and ambled to the doorstep to take in the wood-scented air.

The moon sat there behind wispy clouds, bathing the ancient oaks and sycamores with an eerie glow that seemed to twist their trunks and boughs into evermore bizarre shapes. It was as if, under the stars that peppered heaven's canopy like a scattering of fairy dust, the forest had (snip)

Your verdict? Comments? Edits? Suggestions? Make notes before you turn this page.

Didn't move me on

The writing is nice, but (for me) there's too much of it, as you'll see in a moment. There's what I see as overwriting, and all the detail that takes up so many words slows the pace of this story, and didn't manage to create any tension. After all, nothing much happens other than a woman makes tea and looks out a window.

Notes:

In the kitchen, the kettle was blowing its top like a runaway steam train. (*Suggest "engine" rather than "train."*)

Eliza wrapped a towel around the handle and heaved it from the stove. Wispy curls of steam rose ~~to the ceiling~~ as she poured the boiling water into the ~~waiting~~ teapot, infusing the air with the delicate scent of bergamot. (*"Heaved" bothered me a little—is it that heavy? Also, I'd consider cutting this entire paragraph down to one line to the effect that she poured the boiling water into the teapot. And do you think young adult readers will have any idea what the scent of "bergamot" is? I had to look it up. Adding "orange" as an adjective would help, or "citrus." But I have to wonder what all this fine focus on the tea has to do with the story.*)

~~She left the tea to brew for a moment when s~~ Something **at the window** caught her eye~~, and she automatically looked up. Did~~. **Had** something just pass**ed** by ~~the window~~? Wiping ~~the~~ condensation from the glass, she peered out past the garden to the dark tangled trees of Bracken Wood ~~beyond~~. (*Two "somethings" here. How about "movement" in the first instance?*)

~~Eventually,~~ **Seeing nothing,** she shook her head~~, convincing herself that it was nothing,~~ and poured the Earl Grey into a fine china cup.

A radio babbled away ~~in the background~~, but its half-heard gossip was more a distraction than anything else and she ~~reached over to~~ switch**ed** it off. She **sipped her tea and scalded** ~~raised the cup absently to her mouth to take a sip but ended up scalding~~ her lips. ~~With a wince, she placed the cup back~~ **She winced and set the cup** on the kitchen table and ambled to the doorstep to take in the wood-scented air. *(The "with a wince" doesn't really work because it applies to the action of setting the cup down, not the scalded lips. Also, what does scalding her lips have to do with the story? If her burned lips don't come into play later, you're just spinning your wheels. All this tea stuff, in my view, could be forgotten; I'd jump ahead to the following paragraph after she wipes the condensation off the window. Cut to the chase.)*

The moon sat ~~there~~ behind wispy clouds, bathing ~~the~~ ancient oaks and sycamores with an eerie glow that seemed to twist their trunks and boughs into ~~evermore~~ bizarre shapes. It was as if, under the stars that peppered heaven's canopy like a scattering of fairy dust, the forest had (snip) *(This narrative has much more interesting mood and description than the whole tea adventure, and would do a better job, IMO, in urging the reader on. It promises something. One thing—the words "eerie" and "bizarre" are conclusion words. It's the author deciding what things look like and summarizing. You can use them if you also include description that paints the picture. For example, "bizarre shapes like skeletal giants and hungry ogres.")*

As you know by now, I think the opening page needs to bring some element of tension into the scene as soon as possible. In this case, for example, is there any reason it shouldn't move crisply like this?

In the kitchen, the kettle blew its top like a runaway steam engine. As Ellen poured the boiling water into the teapot, infusing the air with the delicate scent of Earl Grey, something at the window caught her eye.

Wiping condensation from the glass, she peered out past the garden to the dark, tangled trees of Bracken Wood. The moon bathed the ancient oaks and sycamores with a misty glow that seemed to twist their trunks and boughs into bizarre shapes like skeletal giants and hungry ogres.

Rob needs to keep at it, and use that delete key.

Workout 5

Carolyn's first sixteen lines:

A wave of wooziness tells me my blood pressure is dropping. Internal bleeding. It won't be long now. *Focus*, I think, heading through the crowded restaurant to confront Shady Ben Foley and warn his young companions about him. One good deed at the end of my otherwise useless life.

Time slows and details take on a dreamlike clarity: snake charmer music and the spicy smells twine through the air, painted horse heads and bejeweled scabbards decorate the walls, silverware clinks on plates. I'd dragged my boyfriend Cubby into this cheesy Mongolian Restaurant in the course of stalking Foley. My last meal, I think with a rush of grief and terror, nearly tripping over an oriental rug as I avoid colliding with a waiter. It had to come sometime. My condition, known as Vein Star Syndrome, is the proverbial ticking time bomb in the head. Once you're past the point of vascular rupture, no medical attention can save you. Cubby waits back at the table, unaware just how grave my situation has become. I didn't tell him. I didn't want him to stop me from doing this one last decent thing.

"Ben Foley," I say, interrupting their conversation. "Remember me? Pembroke Pines?" I grip the back of an empty chair for support.

Shady Ben gives me this blank look and exchanges bewildered glances with his companions, two blonde men and a pretty girl with long dark ringlets. I remember him so (snip)

Okay, note your verdict and mark up the narrative as needed.

I read on

Good story elements, good writing, and an interesting voice got me to turn the page. There's certainly drama evoked in the first paragraph with her anticipation of dying soon, and then the story immediately adds conflict. Nicely done, Carolyn.

There are a couple of little things that I should note, and a little tightening.

A wave of wooziness tells me my blood pressure is dropping. Internal bleeding. It won't be long now. *Focus*, I think, heading through the crowded restaurant to confront Shady Ben Foley and warn his young companions about him. One good deed at the end of my otherwise useless life.

Time slows and details take on a dreamlike clarity: snake charmer music and ~~the~~ spicy smells twine through the air, painted horse heads and bejeweled scabbards decorate the walls, silverware clinks on plates. I'd dragged my boyfriend Cubby into this cheesy Mongolian Restaurant in the course of stalking Foley. My last meal, I think with a rush of grief and terror~~,~~ ~~nearly tripping over an oriental rug as I avoid colliding with a waiter~~. It had to come sometime. ~~My condition, known as~~ Vein Star Syndrome is the proverbial ticking time bomb in the head. Once you're past the point of vascular rupture, no medical attention can save you. Cubby waits back at the table, unaware **of** just how grave my situation **is** ~~has become~~. I ~~didn't tell~~ **hadn't told** him. I didn't want him to stop me from doing this one last decent thing. *(I like description elements such as "twined through the air.")*

"Ben Foley," I say, interrupting their conversation. "Remember me? Pembroke Pines?" I grip the back of an empty chair for support. *(It's not clear whether "Pembroke Pines" is a person's or a place's name. Could be either. Turns out her name is Justine. I think it should be included here, e.g., "Justine? From Pembroke Pines?")*

Shady Ben gives me this blank look and exchanges bewildered glances with his companions, two **blond** ~~blonde~~ men and a pretty girl with long dark ringlets. I remember him so (snip) *(On "blond:" Common usage is without the "e," though using it is still correct. Some use "blond" for men and "blonde" for women, but I think one consistent spelling is best.)*

There were similar small opportunities for polishing, but overall it was an opening chapter that made me want chapter two. Thanks, Carolyn.

Workout 6

Kim's first sixteen lines:

Michelle Evans burst into SecuraCorp's conference room. "You all need to see this right away."

Blake Barnett didn't have a chance to say a word, let alone stop his cyclone-like secretary from interrupting their Monday, 8 a.m. meeting. He looked across the table at his business partner, Mike Jacobs, sipping a cup of coffee.

Mike grinned and shrugged, as if to say, 'Hey, you hired her pal'.

Blake rose from his chair. "Michelle, we're trying to—"

"Blake, they have someone named Angel."

Mike jumped up. "What?" Coffee sloshed out of his cup and onto the walnut-veneer boardroom table.

Her words took a few seconds to register in Blake's head. *Angel, the world's first cloned human?* Impossible. "That can't be."

"It's true. This arrived special delivery." She handed him a disc enclosed in a clear plastic case.

He snatched what appeared to be a DVD from her hand, and powered up his laptop. "Michelle, would you leave us alone, please?"

Well? Be sure to make notes.

This had virtues, but didn't compel

Virtues include starting with a scene and an effort to create tension and raise story questions. But *(remember, this is subjective)* what happens here didn't grip me or make me really curious about what would happen next.

Parts of the problem include some overwriting and a clarity question. Allow me to get picky in the interests of adding impact.

Michelle Evans burst into SecuraCorp's conference room. "You all need to see this right away." *(Later we learn that she carries something with urgent information on it. Why not get to it now? "This" doesn't give a clue that speaks of importance or jeopardy.)*

Blake Barnett didn't have a chance to say a word, let alone stop his cyclone-like secretary from interrupting their Monday, 8 a.m. meeting. He looked across the table at his business partner, Mike Jacobs, sipping a cup of coffee. *(While I appreciate an effort to characterize the secretary, just how well does this narrative really work? For example, Blake "didn't have a chance to say a word." Actually, he does. She stops speaking. He looks across the table. A sentence from now, he'll stand and say something. So this statement doesn't reflect any kind of reality. I also think this is over-detailed: we don't need to know that this is their Monday, 8 o'clock meeting. We don't need to know at this moment that Mike is his business partner, nor that he's sipping coffee [by the way, he's not sipping "a cup of coffee," he's just sipping coffee—a cup is one helluva sip]. There's information and detail here that doesn't advance the story and, for me, slows things down.)*

Mike grinned and shrugged as if to say, 'Hey, you hired her pal'. *(Now, this really slows things down, and sure doesn't contribute to a sense of urgency, IMO. I'd cut it all.)*

Blake rose from his chair. "Michelle, we're trying to—" *(I suggest "stood" instead of "rose from his chair," which could also mean that he levitated. "Stood" is a nice, specific verb that gives an instant picture. In addition, why are we stalling with Blake's protest?)*

"Blake, they have someone named Angel." *(Now we're getting somewhere—but where? This is still withholding from the reader, and vague. It even uses a vague word, "someone." If the secretary knows enough to tell that whatever it is she holds is urgent, then she knows enough to be specific here.)*

Mike jumped up. "What?" Coffee sloshed out of his cup and onto the walnut-veneer boardroom table. *(You know what I'm going to say, don't you? We don't need to know that the table is "walnut-veneer boardroom." Yes, he jumped up in reaction to her vague announcement. But did we need to slosh coffee? More detail that doesn't contribute to showing us something compelling, in my view.)*

Her words took a few seconds to register in Blake's head. Angel, the world's first cloned human? Impossible. "That can't be." *(Why would the words take a few seconds to register? As we learn later, he was intimately involved in rescuing this cloned girl, so his reaction should have been immediate. More than that, the world's first cloned human is definitely interesting information, yet we don't get to it until now.)*

"It's true. This arrived special delivery." She handed him a disc enclosed in a clear plastic case. *(More ineffective narrative. If she knows what's on the "disc enclosed in a clear plastic case," then why the heck didn't she say so up front instead of all this dancing around? As for "disc enclosed in a clear plastic case," this is cautious over-explaining. She knows it's a DVD—she has to have viewed it to know what's on it—so why not have her say what it is?)*

He snatched what appeared to be a DVD from her hand and powered up his laptop. "Michelle, would you leave us alone, please?" *(As just pointed out, we should already know that this is a DVD. The "what appeared" is more cautious description. Why does he ask to be alone if she already knows what's on the DVD? This opening to a thriller/suspense novel needs to let 'er rip, not dance around. In my view, that is.)*

The story that develops could be interesting, but the delivery continued to need work, with more detail than needed and some info-dumping. How could this opening have been stronger? Here's a quick rewrite:

Blake Barnet's secretary burst into the meeting. "Angel's been kidnapped." Michelle handed him a computer disk. "This DVD just came."

Blake said, "Dammit!" Even though people tended to think of the first human clone as an object, Angel was just a little girl with big, sad eyes. He loaded the disk in his laptop while his partner Mike hurried around the table.

Now we have the clone aspect in, plus a strong hint that he has a connection with her. I hope this illustrates how Kim could have spent her narrative hooking me on the drama of her story instead of filling me in on tabletops and coffee spills. And this version took only five lines of narrative.

Workout 7

The first sixteen lines of Greg's fantasy novel:

To tell the truth, Dora Faye didn't know whether she was about to kill herself or not. All her life she'd wanted to be spontaneous and creative, open to all the sweetly surprising spin-on-the-head-of-a-pin possibilities of life — especially now with regards to the ending of it — and tonight she figured she'd just go with the flow. *Live or die, oh me oh my. Maybe yes, maybe no. Easy come, easy go. Tra la la la la.* But one thing was for damn sure. She wanted a corndog. The carnival was in town.

On this sticky June night her mind played tricks on her. Snowflakes danced over the Ferris wheel. Since snowflakes don't have a mind of their own to zig and zag, flit and flap independently, this made no sense at all to Dora Faye. *Snow in June?*

Her nostrils flared as a frypit breeze of onions and peppers—greasy with diesel fumes—teased her brunette hair. She'd chopped it to try for a more youthful image before they snipped her American Express; suddenly lacking the plastic cash for the nip 'n' tucks to firm up the face, the pageboy thing just wasn't working at all for her.

As she drove her Delta 88 ragtop into the parking lot and killed the ignition, her ears caught a muddy wave of pop tunes, punched out by worn-out carny speakers, as they and her Top 40 regrets washed through her mind.

Turn? Notes for this writer?

Opening and voice moved me on

Nice voice here, and fun writing for the most part. I did read on, and have a note later for Greg about that. This opening, thanks to the first paragraph, raises a strong story question. Some notes:

~~To tell the truth,~~ Dora Faye didn't know whether she was about to kill herself or not. All her life she'd wanted to be spontaneous and creative, open to all the sweetly surprising spin-on-the-head-of-a-pin possibilities of life—especially now with regards to the ending of it—and tonight she figured she'd just go with the flow. *Live or die, oh me oh my. Maybe yes, maybe no. Easy come, easy go. Tra la la la la.* But one thing was for damn sure. She wanted a corndog. ~~The carnival was in town.~~ *(Except for the first phrase, I really liked this. The contrast between the death wish and the corn dog craving was engaging. I cut the "truth" phrase because it seems a shame to begin such an interesting piece of narrative with a tired old phrase. Wasn't needed, either, IMO. I cut the line about the carnival because the corndog was such a surprise and nifty ending for the paragraph. I've added the carnival later)*

On this sticky June night her mind played tricks on her. Snowflakes danced over the **carnival** Ferris wheel. Since snowflakes ~~don't~~ **didn't** have a mind of their own to zig and zag, flit and flap independently, ~~this~~ **that** made no sense at all to Dora Faye. *Snow in June? (The first sentence steps out of her point of view and into the author's. In a close third person POV, she wouldn't be thinking about a sticky June night in this way. And "her mind played tricks on her" is telling rather than showing. Thought-starter: begin with the snowflakes part. Then, instead of the "Snow in June" internal monologue, carry on with the no sense thing at the end to describe the night, i.e.,* Neither did snowflakes on a sticky June night.*)*

Her nostrils flared ~~as~~ **when** a fry-pit breeze of onions and peppers—greasy with diesel fumes—teased her ~~brunette~~ hair. She'd chopped it to try for a more youthful image before they snipped her American Express; suddenly lacking the plastic cash for the nip-'n'-tucks to firm up the face, the pageboy thing just wasn't working at all for her. *(Stating the color of her hair is another slip in POV—unless she's looking at it in a mirror (a rear-view mirror, in this case), she wouldn't be thinking about the color. I liked the "fry-pit breeze" part, but that leads to an inconsistency in the next paragraph. I think this description could be cut or moved to later.)*

~~As~~ **After** she drove her Delta 88 ragtop into the parking lot and killed the ignition, her ears caught a muddy wave of pop tunes, punched out by worn-out carny speakers as ~~they and~~ her Top 40 regrets washed through her mind. *(This may be totally subjective, but...while "ragtop" is a good synonym for convertible, it created an image of a convertible with the top up (because of "top"). Turns out the top is down. Here's a staging problem: in the previous paragraph, before we know she's in a convertible with the top down, she smells odors on the breeze. Yet at that point she isn't in the parking lot by the carnival, as we learn here. Rethink the order of things here. I'd get her into the parking lot first, stop the car, and then let the breeze do its thing. And if she's driving, the air flow of a top-down convertible would defeat any breeze. Also, I wouldn't have her ears catch the music; keep it simple, i.e. "She caught a muddy wave...etc.)*

Good stuff.

Workout 8

Marty's first sixteen lines:

Temperance Jones struggles into her winter coat. She has not even bothered to remove her nightgown. In the last few years she has simply begun to put her clothes over the top of it. Stockings cover her thin legs and a long wool skirt hangs well past her knees. She starts looking for her gloves. She knows they aren't very far away but at 73 her mind has began to wonder and her memory isn't so good anymore. Still she needs to find her gloves without them her hands will be covered with blisters by the end of the day. Temperance has dug all day without them in the past, so she is well aware of the consequences. She spots them lying on top of her boots. Guiltily she looks around the room as she picks them up, almost like she expects someone to be watching and judging her failing memory. But of course she is alone.

Temperance has considered replacing her stockings with slacks like her family has suggested. They would definitely keep her legs warm but she couldn't bring herself to do it. Ladies didn't wear trousers. She had heard that numerous times from her mother when she was a child. Her sweet mother had always been the very picture of what a lady should be. Even when she was found dead at the bottom of the stairs she had managed to fall in a ladylike position. Temperance wondered what her mother would think of her if she were alive today. If she could see everything that she has done and worse everything that has been done to her over the years. Would she still (snip)

Make notes!

I stalled out on backstory

I liked the voice, and the point of view of a seventy-three-year-old is definitely interesting. I was even willing to go along with the leisurely tone, but for me there was finally too much doddering old lady stuff and not enough hint of an interesting story at hand.

That's the danger of dawdling on an opening page. Shortly thereafter, Mary had this line:

Ladies don't wear trousers but they don't get gang raped and smother the life out of their elderly husbands either.

That raised interesting story questions, but too late. And then the narrative dropped into backstory. For me, there just wasn't enough tension. And there were a few craft problems. My notes:

Temperance Jones struggles into her winter coat. She has not even bothered to remove her nightgown. In the last few years**,** she has simply ~~begun to~~ put her clothes over the top of it. Stockings cover her thin legs and a wool skirt hangs well past her knees. She ~~starts looking~~ **looks** for her gloves. She knows they aren't very far away**,** but at ~~73~~ **seventy-three** her mind has ~~began~~ **begun** to ~~wonder~~ **wander** and her memory isn't so good anymore. Still**,** she needs to find her gloves**;** without them her hands will be covered with blisters by the end of the day. ~~Temperance has dug all day without them in the past, so she is well aware of the consequences.~~ She spots them lying on top of her boots. ~~Guiltily~~ She looks around the room as ~~she picks them up, almost like she expects~~ **if** someone **were** ~~to be~~ watching and judging her failing memory. But of course she is alone. *(There were a few comma faults, and one missing semi-colon. I think little misses like that rob narrative of the professional tone it must have, as does the occasional misspelled word [wander]. The part about "Stockings cover her thin legs" steps away from her point of view and tells rather than shows. I think you could communicate thin legs descriptively, e.g., "Baggy stockings cover her legs…")*

Temperance has considered replacing her stockings with slacks like her family has suggested. They would definitely keep her legs warm, but she ~~couldn't~~ **can't** bring herself to do it. Ladies ~~didn't~~ **don't** wear trousers. She had heard that numerous times from her mother when she was a child. Her sweet mother had always been the very picture of what a lady should be. Even when she was found dead at the bottom of the stairs, she had managed to fall in a ladylike position. ~~Temperance wondered what her mother would think of her if she were alive today. If she could see everything that she has done and worse everything that has been done to her over the years. Would she still~~ (snip) *(An opening is not time, IMO, for a character to slip into rumination. Eliminate that and we get to the gang rape/smothering part on the first page.)*

It seems like there could definitely be something intriguing here, and the voice is strong. Work on tightening the narrative and keeping the focus on what's happening will make us want to know what happens next.

Workout 9

This workout is a little different. It's a longer sample (about two manuscript pages) of good writing that can be made better. So here's your workout: go through and do your best to edit, make notes, etc. Indicate moving text around if you see a need, do whatever it takes to improve the narrative.

Every small town has its secrets. Dirty things. Growing up in Dark Hills, I thought I knew them all. Then I learned different.

#

Elise has the gift of truth. Say something to her, or in front of her, and she knows if you're lying or not. It don't go no further than that. She can't see the past or future. Grams could, when she was alive. That, and so much more. But each generation inherited less and less of her abilities, a dilution of genetics. Momma tried her best to pass something along to us. She married her cousin, kept everything in the family. Her brother did the same. That's where Elise came from.

Maybe we'll have better luck.

#

I didn't pay much mind when Daisy brought home that first bone. Labradors always bring home shit to chew on, and Daisy ain't no exception. It wasn't even a big piece. I was more nervous about Daisy choking than I was about touching it. So it was more surprise than actual pain made me yelp when I pulled it from her mouth.

"Ow! Goddamn!" I dropped the bone onto the porch, quickly covered it with my foot before Daisy could snatch it up. I was wearing shoes so I didn't worry about getting shocked again.

"Kip? Somethin' wrong?" Elise called from the kitchen.

"Nothin,'" And it was true. "Daisy brought in a chunk of bone and it buzzed me when I touched it."

"And why'd you touch it in the first place?" She came to the top step and leaned against the railing, crossing her summer-tanned arms and staring at me. A calculated pose, flirting. She knew it would push up her breasts so they was close to bustin' out of her old denim shirt.

As always, her beauty caught me like a squirrel in a trap. I know what you're thinking, but things is different in Dark Hills. We ain't the first set of cousins to take up together. Most families try to discourage it, while ours always had a preference for it.

If you'd ever seen Elise, you wouldn't blame me. At fifteen she'd had a body and face to rival any actress on the covers of the magazines down to the supermarket. At twenty-one she looked even better.

Me, I wasn't quite as blessed. Better than average looks, or so I've been told, but with a price. I guess you'd call it a deformity. Extra middle finger on each hand, longer than the others. Extra toes to match. Elise says it's the extra fingers make me sensitive to the bones.

I bent down, gingerly touching the small, gray shard. No buzz, no sudden visions. Feeling more secure, I picked it up and showed it to her. "It's all right. Normally I wouldn't have felt a thing, but whatever it came from must have died in a lotta pain."

Elise's amber-hued eyes widened. "Was it a person?"

"Can't tell," I juggled the shard back and forth. "But I doubt it. Prob'ly a deer that got itself shot, or maybe hit by a car. It died in the woods and Daisy found the remains."

"Well, be careful next time," Elise poked me with a finger. "I don't want you passin' out and knockin' yourself senseless, 'specially if I ain't around."

"That was one time." I stuck the bone in my shirt pocket. "I ain't ten no more."

"You ain't?" she asked with a little grin.

I know an invitation when I see it, and I accepted. Like I said, it may seem wrong to you, but you haven't met Elise.

This is good stuff

It definitely has "voice," to my ear a likeable one. From a story point of view, it offers me a visit to a world unknown to me, which creates strong appeal. But there's work to be done. Here's how I'd edit this piece:

~~Every small town has its secrets. Dirty things. Growing up in Dark Hills, I thought I knew them all. Then I learned different.~~ *(I suggest you start with story. Next, I moved the paragraphs about Elise to later because the reader doesn't know who she is. I think the paragraph that follows is your opening. It starts with action and raises an alluring story question.)*

I didn't pay much mind when Daisy brought home **the** ~~that~~ first bone. Labradors always bring home shit to chew on, and Daisy ain't no exception. It wasn't even a big piece. ~~I was more nervous about Daisy choking than I was about touching it.~~ So it was more surprise than actual pain made me yelp when I pulled it from her mouth. *(I think this creates a much more suspenseful opening because it has the reader wondering about the bone. There are more bones to come, right? I'm assuming that it is significant. I cut the one sentence because it didn't really add, and there was a use for the choking part later.)*

"~~Ow!~~ Goddamn!" I dropped the bone onto the porch and ~~quickly~~ covered it with my foot before Daisy could snatch it up. I was wearing shoes so I didn't worry about getting shocked again. *(Note on dog's name: it could be a person's name, too. Considering the rural aspect of these characters, maybe a name that wouldn't be human would avoid potential confusion.)*

Elise called from the kitchen. "Kip? Somethin' wrong?" **She's my cousin, and a whole bunch more.** *(Note shift of action in the first sentence from back to front to let reader know who is speaking and from where. Due to moving the paragraph that introduces the nature of their relationship to later in the narrative, I suggested adding the last sentence so what's to come will make sense.)*

"Nothin'." And it was true. "Daisy brought in a chunk of bone and it buzzed me when I touched it."

"And why'd you touch it in the first place?" She came to the top step and leaned against the railing, crossing her summer-tanned arms and staring at me. A calculated pose, flirting. She knew it would push up her breasts so they was close to bustin' out of her old denim shirt.

As always, her beauty caught me like a squirrel in a trap. I know what you're thinking, but things is different in Dark Hills. We ain't the first set of cousins to take up together. Most families try to discourage it, while ours always had a preference for it. *(I think this paragraph should start with an answer to her question, i.e., "'Fraid she'd choke on it." Otherwise it seems like he's ignoring it.)*

If you~~'d~~ ever ~~seen~~ **saw** Elise, you wouldn't blame me. At fifteen she'd had a body and face to rival any actress on the covers of the magazines down to the supermarket. At twenty-one she looked even better. *(A little ambiguous on her age, doesn't really say how old she is now because sentence could refer to earlier. A solution:* Now, at twenty-one, she looked even better.*)*

Elise has the gift of truth. Say something ~~to her, or~~ in front of her~~,~~ and she knows if you're lying or not. It don't go no further than that. She can't see the past or future. Grams could, when she was alive. That, and so much more. But each generation inherited less and less of her abilities, a dilution of genetics. Momma tried her best to pass something along to us. She married her cousin, kept everything in the family. Her brother did the same. That's where Elise came from.

Maybe we'll have better luck. *(Moved these previous two paragraphs to here so you don't have readers wondering who the hell Elise is in the opening, and the information about her comes with the introduction to her.)*

Me, I wasn't quite as blessed. Better than average looks, or so I've been told, but with a price. I guess you'd call it a deformity. Extra middle finger on each hand, longer than the others. Extra toes to match. Elise says it's the extra fingers make me sensitive to the bones.

I bent down, gingerly touching the small, gray shard. *(This sentence says he touched the shard as he bent down, but that's not right. More accurately: "I bent down and gingerly touched...")* No buzz, no sudden visions. ~~Feeling more secure,~~ I picked it up and showed it to her. "It's all right. Normally I wouldn't have felt a thing, but whatever it came from must have died in a lotta pain."

Elise's amber-hued eyes widened. "Was it a person?"

"Can't tell." I juggled the shard back and forth. ~~But I doubt it.~~ "Prob'ly a deer that got itself shot, or maybe hit by a car. It died in the woods and Daisy found the remains."

"Well, be careful next time." Elise poked me with a finger. "I don't want you passin' out and knockin' yourself senseless, 'specially if I ain't around."

"That was one time." I stuck the bone in my shirt pocket. "I ain't ten no more." *(nice use of backstory and avoiding a flashback.)*

"You ain't?" she asked with a little grin.

I know an invitation when I see it, and I accepted. Like I said, it may seem wrong to you, but you haven't met Elise.

I'd like more on the sights, sounds and scents of the scene, but that's about it. Promising stuff. I'd sure keep turning the pages.

I find it difficult to compare the before and after in this form, so next you'll find the two narratives side by side, with the edited version on the left.

Which opening paragraphs engage you with something happening?

Which narrative tracks smoothest, goes down easiest?

Edited version

I didn't pay much mind when Daisy brought home the first bone. Labradors always bring home shit to chew on, and Daisy ain't no exception. It wasn't even a big piece. So it was more surprise than actual pain made me yelp when I pulled it from her mouth.

"Goddamn!" I dropped the bone onto the porch and covered it with my foot before Daisy could snatch it up. I was wearing shoes, so I didn't worry about getting shocked again.

Elise called from the kitchen. "Kip? Somethin' wrong?" She's my cousin, and a whole bunch more.

"Nothin'." And it was true. "Daisy brought in a chunk of bone and it buzzed me when I touched it."

"And why'd you touch it in the first place?" She came to the top step and leaned against the railing, crossing her summer-tanned arms and staring at me. A calculated pose, flirting. She knew it would push up her breasts so they was close to bustin' out of her old denim shirt.

"Fraid she'd choke on it." As always, her beauty caught me like a squirrel in a trap. I know what you're thinking, but things is different in Dark Hills. We ain't the first set of cousins to take up together. Most families try to discourage it, while ours always had a preference for it.

If you ever saw Elise, you wouldn't blame me. At fifteen she'd had a body and face to rival any actress on the covers of the magazines down to the supermarket. Now, at twenty-one, she looked even better.

Elise has the gift of truth. Say something in front of her and she knows if you're lying or not. It don't go no further than that. She can't see the past or future. Grams could, when she was alive. That, and so much more. But each generation

(continued)

Original

Every small town has its secrets. Dirty things. Growing up in Dark Hills, I thought I knew them all. Then I learned different.

#

Elise has the gift of truth. Say something to her, or in front of her, and she knows if you're lying or not. It don't go no further than that. She can't see the past or future. Grams could, when she was alive. That, and so much more. But each generation inherited less and less of her abilities, a dilution of genetics. Momma tried her best to pass something along to us. She married her cousin, kept everything in the family. Her brother did the same. That's where Elise came from.

Maybe we'll have better luck.

#

I didn't pay much mind when Daisy brought home that first bone. Labradors always bring home shit to chew on, and Daisy ain't no exception. It wasn't even a big piece. I was more nervous about Daisy choking than I was about touching it. So it was more surprise than actual pain made me yelp when I pulled it from her mouth.

"Ow! Goddamn!" I dropped the bone onto the porch, quickly covered it with my foot before Daisy could snatch it up. I was wearing shoes so I didn't worry about getting shocked again.

"Kip? Somethin' wrong?" Elise called from the kitchen.

"Nothin,'" And it was true. "Daisy brought in a chunk of bone and it buzzed me when I touched it."

"And why'd you touch it in the first place?" She came to the top step and leaned against the railing, crossing her summer-tanned arms and staring at me. A calculated pose, flirting. She knew it would push up her breasts so they was close to bustin' out of her old denim shirt.

(continued)

Edited version

inherited less and less of her abilities, a dilution of genetics. Momma tried her best to pass something along to us. She married her cousin, kept everything in the family. Her brother did the same. That's where Elise came from.

Maybe we'll have better luck.

Me, I wasn't quite as blessed as her. Better than average looks, or so I've been told, but with a price. I guess you'd call it a deformity. Extra middle finger on each hand, longer than the others. Extra toes to match. Elise says it's the extra fingers make me sensitive to the bones.

I bent down and gingerly touched the small, gray shard. No buzz, no sudden visions. I picked it up and showed it to her. "It's all right. Normally I wouldn't have felt a thing, but whatever it came from must have died in a lotta pain."

Elise's amber-hued eyes widened. "Was it a person?"

"Can't tell." I juggled the shard back and forth. "Prob'ly a deer that got itself shot, or maybe hit by a car. It died in the woods and Daisy found the remains."

"Well, be careful next time." Elise poked me with a finger. "I don't want you passin' out and knockin' yourself senseless, 'specially if I ain't around."

"That was one time." I stuck the bone in my shirt pocket. "I ain't ten no more."

"You ain't?" she asked with a little grin.

I know an invitation when I see it, and I accepted. Like I said, it may seem wrong to you, but you haven't met Elise.

Original

As always, her beauty caught me like a squirrel in a trap. I know what you're thinking, but things is different in Dark Hills. We ain't the first set of cousins to take up together. Most families try to discourage it, while ours always had a preference for it.

If you'd ever seen Elise, you wouldn't blame me. At fifteen she'd had a body and face to rival any actress on the covers of the magazines down to the supermarket. At twenty-one she looked even better.

Me, I wasn't quite as blessed. Better than average looks, or so I've been told, but with a price. I guess you'd call it a deformity. Extra middle finger on each hand, longer than the others. Extra toes to match. Elise says it's the extra fingers make me sensitive to the bones.

I bent down, gingerly touching the small, gray shard. No buzz, no sudden visions. Feeling more secure, I picked it up and showed it to her. "It's all right. Normally I wouldn't have felt a thing, but whatever it came from must have died in a lotta pain."

Elise's amber-hued eyes widened. "Was it a person?"

"Can't tell," I juggled the shard back and forth. "But I doubt it. Prob'ly a deer that got itself shot, or maybe hit by a car. It died in the woods and Daisy found the remains."

"Well, be careful next time," Elise poked me with a finger. "I don't want you passin' out and knockin' yourself senseless, 'specially if I ain't around."

"That was one time." I stuck the bone in my shirt pocket. "I ain't ten no more."

"You ain't?" she asked with a little grin.

I know an invitation when I see it, and I accepted. Like I said, it may seem wrong to you, but you haven't met Elise.

Workout 10

Another longer sample of an opening, this one from a first draft of a novella by a published author, Joe Nassise, author of the *Templar Chronicles* trilogy. He's very good, but there are small issues that can be addressed to make this opening even better. Keeping in mind the six elements of good stories, go through and do your best to edit, make notes, etc.

In the moment after midnight, the world held its breath.

Like a finely-tuned watch in need of attention, time slowed, and then stopped. One moment the truck stop was full of noise and activity, in the next everything came to a halt.

In the sudden silence, I looked up from my late-night meal of eggs and hash to find the room around me frozen in time. A few tables away, the lithesome teen who moments before had been haranguing her bull-necked boyfriend in righteous anger now stood with her finger pointed at his chest, one hip cocked jauntily as if in unintended invitation. The waitress, a plump matronly woman with too much makeup and a quick, easy smile, had been caught in the act of pouring another cup of coffee for the bearded trucker at the end of the breakfast counter, the liquid suspended in mid-air like a wave on the verge of breaking. The highway patrol officer who'd just hustled in from the parking lot stood halfway between the dining area and the bathroom, one foot suspended inches above the floor.

Even the clock on the wall had stopped, silenced at 30 seconds after twelve.

Everyone, and everything, was still.

Except me.

The sense of *déjà vu* I experienced in the next moment was almost overwhelming. I had seen this place before; I knew what was coming next.

And it scared the piss out of me.

Before the thought had fully formed I was up and moving, scrambling away from the weary family in the booth behind me, getting out in the center of the room where my options increased and the chance of collateral damage to those around me would be minimized.

As I moved I kept my attention firmly on the long stretch of mirror that covered the wall behind the breakfast counter. Even as I watched, it grew smoke-dark and frost began to form at its edges.

Too late!

A face swam into view in the glass; long and gaunt, with sunken eyes and hollowed cheeks, a face of winter grey capped by strands of writhing hair that twitched and moved with life all their own.

Its empty eyes pinned me with the inerrancy of a laser.

Snarling silently, the chimera pierced the Veil and reached toward me. The mirror's surface seemed to ripple and shiver, the creature's hand passing through it without resistance, and then the chimera pulled itself into our world, the glass behind it going solid with a sharp snap. Without hesitation the creature leaped for me.

The gun I'd taken off the dead cop in Toledo was out before the beast had cleared the counter, the thunder of the weapon's voice echoing in the confines of the room. My shots struck it full in the face, tossing it backward to the floor like so much discarded garbage, but I knew it wouldn't be down for long.

After facing them three times, I still had no idea how to kill these things.

Motion caught my eye and my gaze shifted back to the mirror just as several more faces began to form inside the darkened glass. My arm lifted slightly, my finger twitched, and another shot shattered the mirror's surface, closing that exit from the Road.

I knew it would only take the reinforcements a few moments to find another portal. Every moment counted. Even the tiniest advantage might mean the difference between life and death and I didn't intend to waste a bit of it.

The truck stop was too confining; I'd have a better chance of survival outside, in the open, so I headed for the door, snatching the satchel off the seat next to me on my way.

Things had started going crazy five weeks ago, when she came to me in my dreams for the first time. Eyes of green and hair that deep blue-black that seems almost iridescent in certain light. She was standing off in the distance, yelling, but I was unable to understand what she was saying. Each night her image grew steadily clearer, those two almond shapes eyes staring out of a hazy profile that grew more distinct with each passing day, until I could recognize the expression of fear and pain on her otherwise gorgeous face. That night, I'd heard her voice clearly for the first time.

"Run!" she'd said.

Whew! Strong stuff for a first draft. Joe uses all the elements of a good story to hook us and keep the pages turning. Note how Joe's use of short paragraphs creates a fast-moving pace and a sense of action. But even this writing can use tightening, clarification, and thought about word choice—after all, it's a first draft. Following are my notes for Joe's work.

In the moment after midnight, the world held its breath. *(Nice. Immediately creates a mood of suspense.)*

Like a finely~~-~~tuned watch *(an adjective modified by an adverb is generally not hyphenated. As a general rule, adverbs ending in –ly don't need hyphens when they immediately precede the word they modify. I have struggled with this myself, retraining my instincts.)* in need of attention, time slowed, and then stopped. One moment the truck stop was full of noise and activity, in the next everything came to a halt.

In the sudden silence, I looked up from my late-night meal of eggs and hash to find the room around me frozen in time. A few tables away, the lithesome teen who moments before had been haranguing her bull-necked boyfriend in righteous anger now stood with her finger pointed at his chest, one hip cocked jauntily as if in unintended invitation. The waitress, a plump matronly woman with too much makeup and a quick, easy smile, had been <u>caught in the act</u> of pouring **a** ~~another~~ cup of coffee for the bearded trucker at the end of the breakfast counter, the liquid suspended in midair like a wave on the verge of breaking. *(A couple of things: the phrase "caught in the act" is a cliché; you can do better. And "caught" is a little ambiguous here, for me, anyway. Maybe something more evocative, such as: had become a statue pouring a cup of...etc.)* The highway patrol officer who'd just hustled in from the parking lot stood halfway between the dining area and the bathroom, one foot suspended inches above the floor.

Even the clock on the wall had stopped, silenced at ~~30~~ **thirty** seconds after twelve. *(Question: Do smells still happen in frozen time? The scent of the hash browns or coffee, etc.? Can they be added to flesh out the experience?)*

Everyone, and everything, was still. *(How about adding a reference to the utter silence that would also occur?)*

Except me.

The sense of déjà vu I experienced in the next moment was almost overwhelming. ~~I had seen this place before;~~ I knew what was coming next.

And it scared the piss out of me.

Before the thought had fully formed I was up and moving, scrambling away from the weary family in the booth behind me, getting out in the center of the room where my options increased and the chance of collateral damage to those around me would be minimized.

As I moved I kept my attention firmly on the long stretch of mirror that covered the wall behind the breakfast counter. Even as I watched, it grew smoke-dark and frost began to form at its edges. *(nice)*

Too late!

A face swam into view *(bit of a cliché)* in the glass; long and gaunt, with sunken eyes and hollowed cheeks, a face of winter grey capped by strands of writhing hair that twitched and moved with life all their own.

~~Its e~~ Empty eyes pinned me with the inerrancy of a laser. *(Technically, this "its" refers to the hair, not the face. Suggest you just delete the "its:" i.e. "Empty eyes pinned me...")*

Snarling silently *(Actually, a snarl is a sound, so it can't really be silent. maybe something else, like "its face twisted with a snarl")*, the chimera pierced the Veil and reached toward me. The mirror's surface seemed to ripple and shiver *(Why "seemed to"? Why not "The mirror's surface rippled and shivered...")*, the creature's hand passing through it ~~without resistance~~, and then the chimera pulled itself into our world, the glass behind it going solid with a sharp snap. *("Going solid" makes my case for getting rid of "seemed to" earlier; here the glass reverts to what it was before rippling and shivering, right? Also, how does he know that there's no resistance? A small POV slip.)* Without hesitation the creature leaped for me. *(You*

226

can do without the "without"—just have the creature leap. Also, I could use a little more picture here. Remind me that it's behind the counter. Did it spring over the counter from a standing position, or did it place a hand on the bar and vault over? Help me see what it does. Also, does it wear clothes? You've described the face, but what about the rest of it? Tall? Muscular?)

The gun I'd taken off the dead cop in Toledo was out before the beast had cleared the counter. *(Passive. Maybe something like: "I had the gun I'd taken off the dead cop in Toledo out before..." However, this is an excellent way to work a bit of backstory in without slowing the train.)* the thunder of the weapon's voice echoing in the confines of the room. My shots struck it full in the face, tossing it backward to the floor like so much discarded garbage, *(Since this is horror, don't you think a little more gore would be good here? Just a touch?)* but I knew it wouldn't be down for long.

After facing them three times, I still had no idea how to kill these things.

Motion caught my eye and my gaze shifted back to the mirror just as several more *("Several" is vague, abstract—why not tell us how many? Specific details create a reality. I imagine four.)* faces began to form inside the darkened glass. My arm lifted ~~slightly~~, my finger twitched, and ~~another~~ **my** shot shattered the mirror's surface, closing that exit from the Road. *(Cool.)*

I knew it would only take the reinforcements a few moments to find another portal. *(He can't really know. How about: "Every other time it had taken only moments for reinforcements to find another portal.")* Every ~~single~~ moment counted. Even the tiniest advantage might mean the difference between life and death, and I didn't intend to waste a bit of it.

The truck stop was too confining; I'd have a better chance of survival ~~outside~~ in the open, so I headed for the door, snatching the satchel off the seat next to me ~~on my way~~.

Things had started going crazy five weeks ago, when she came to me in my dreams for the first time. Eyes of green and hair of that deep blue-black that seems almost iridescent in certain light. She was standing off in the distance, yelling, but I was unable to understand what she was saying. Each night her image grew steadily clearer, those two almond-shaped eyes staring out of a hazy profile *(If her face is in profile there would be only one eye visible.)* that grew more distinct with each passing day, until I could recognize the expression of fear and pain on her otherwise gorgeous face. ~~That~~ **On that** night, I'd heard her voice clearly for the first time.

"Run!" she'd said.

How did your edits/notes compare? In a paid edit I might get even pickier, but realistically, there's not much to pick at, is there?

Creating distance for better self-editing

You've just spent some time editing the work of other writers, and perhaps found it easy to spot shortcomings. But if you're like most of us, it's far more difficult to see your own shortcomings with any clarity, if at all.

To self-edit with any success, create distance from your work to somehow separate your reading from your intimate knowledge of your vision so that the words alone do the work. With distance, it falls on the writing to evoke scenes no longer fresh in your mind. Not so amazingly, distance reveals holes in the pictures. And flat writing becomes visible for the first time, those lazy word choices or adverbs that got you through the task of getting the story down but don't do diddly-squat to create the reader experience you need to provoke.

Once done with a draft, try not to go back for at least a month, though six weeks is better. However, unless I have other projects interesting enough to distract me, I find that very difficult to do. A few days go by and then, like a constant itch that needs scratching, I open the file and start picking. Compulsive, I know, but I don't see how anyone could write an entire novel without a healthy dose of compulsive behavior to keep giving the wheel a turn when you have a tough day.

So I needed to find other ways to get around the fact that I refused to allow my book adequate time to chill. Here are some that might work for you.

You could do as George Carlin once talked of doing in the last stages of polishing his material—smoke a little pot. Failing that, what?

If you've been working exclusively onscreen, create a printout and go through a hard copy. That's a must at some time anyway, and it can gain you a little psychological distance.

Read it aloud to yourself. For me, this reveals clumsy structure; unwanted repetitions and echoes; missing information; too much information; or other flaws. I don't do this often enough, probably because I simply forget to.

Another technique that works for me is to reformat the narrative to look more like that in a book. Here are ways to do that using Microsoft Word (this is doable in WordPerfect as well).

1. Change the font.

If you're using Courier, it'll never look like a book. Times New Roman is closer in appearance to a book's text, but it's a narrow newspaper font seldom used in a book. And it would be better to eye a different font anyway.

To change the font, type Ctrl+a (or Apple+a with a Mac). This should select all the text. Then go to the font window in your toolbar and change it to one of the book-style fonts: Garamond or Palatino or Georgia, if you have them. If you don't, Times New Roman will do. Font size: 12.

Author M.J. Rose, *The Halo Effect*, prints her manuscript out in a different font and then takes it somewhere else to read—2 or 3 hours a day at a library, or on a train from Connecticut to Boston and back all in one day. I like that idea—your words have to overcome unaccustomed distractions. And a different environment can make you see things in different ways.

2. Make the text even more look book-like

While you've still got everything selected (or do Ctrl+a again to select all), change the spacing to be more book-like as well, neither double nor single spacing. Click Format>Paragraph. In the Line Spacing box, use the dropdown menu to select Multiple. Then, in the "At:" box next to it, type 1.1 or 1.2 and click OK. Adjust to taste. Another way to do it is use point size. Choose "Exactly" and enter in a larger point size. For 12-point type, 15 will give you a more open, book-like feel than single spacing. But you're not done yet.

Change the margins to create a bookish column of text on the page with about 10-15 words in a line. The margins I've found helpful are: top, 1"; bottom, 1"; left and right, 1.7". This will give you a very different look.

3. Make it look like a book.

It's fun to really go all the way and see how it would look book-style by doing this:

1. Change the page size. Click File>Page setup and go to the Paper size tab. Change the paper size to Custom and type in 5.5" for width and 8.5" for height. Or 6" by 9".

2. Now change the margins: top, .66"; bottom, left, and right to .6".

3. Change the font and spacing as noted above. Might try a smaller font size, 11.5 or 11, depending on the font.

4. Justify the margins. Select all the text (Ctrl+a). Click Format>Paragraph. On the Indents and Spacing tab, go to the Alignment box, click the arrow to show the menu, and choose Justified. Then click OK.

I think you'll find that the reformatted narrative reads differently, either onscreen or in a printout. I've even printed out a book on 5.5" by 8.5" paper, using both sides of the paper and formatting just like a book (headers, page numbers, justified margins, font, spacing, etc.), and had it tape-bound at Kinko's, which yielded something very much like a perfect-bound trade paperback. Now, that's fun to hold in your hands—your book as a real book! It's educational, too.

Have trouble working in standard manuscript format?

These ideas on creating distance solved a problem I've never had for a writer named Janine. She wrote this after discovering my tip on reformatting.

> I have a HUGE problem working in traditional manuscript format (12 pt courier double spaced ragged right margin etc.) I find it very distracting and get lost easily. I end up with these ENORMOUS drafts that are too intimidating to revise.
>
> I decided I was just going to set up my working draft like a book page and "write the book" while I do the draft. It's an amazingly powerful tool. I know right where I am in the story. No more guessing. I know that when I'm finally done I'll have to reformat it for submission but hey, who cares? At least this way I might get a finished draft TO submit. Before, it was looking kind of hopeless.

For what it's worth.

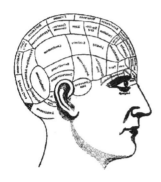

Section 7: Computer tips

You may already know about the following uses of features found in Word and WordPerfect, but I know that they are news to some writers. I've found that the Bookmarks and Comments features can be of great help while writing a first draft and in revisions.

Computer tip
Make writing more productive with bookmarks

First, keep the entire book manuscript in one electronic file—it's a huge time-saver. I know writers who use a separate file on their computer for each chapter of their book. Each of my novels is in one file—the whole thing. It would drive me nuts to have to open up, let's say, a file for chapter 9 in order to check on information I needed for a scene in chapter 22—for example, maybe I need to make sure where I stashed a clue back in chapter 9 that now needs to be discovered in 22.

A file-per-chapter writer friend didn't see how I could do it. The key is using bookmarks to navigate quickly and easily around a complete novel manuscript.

With the Microsoft Word and WordPerfect Bookmark tools, wherever you are in a manuscript you can insert a bookmark and easily come back to it from any other place in the manuscript. I used it frequently in putting this book together to jump from where I was writing to a previous section to check on something in another section. I'd insert the letter "a" as a bookmark where I was, go to where I needed to go, and then just use the bookmark to hop back. I use "a" because it comes up at the top of the bookmark list. And you can use it over and over—when I needed to do the same thing further on in the manuscript, the "a" was at the top of the list and it was simple to just select it, click "insert," and have the "a" bookmark located in the new place.

Another use for bookmarks is when you're deep into rewriting or polishing your book and it's time to hang up your brain for the night, your eyes having become loose in their sockets. If you're on, let's say, line 16 on page 174 out of 263, the quick way to return to that exact spot is insert a bookmark—the letter "a" will do, or perhaps "here," or whatever is easiest—save the file, and shut down. Next day, you can return to the exact spot you left off with a couple of keystrokes.

In Word you click Insert; click Bookmark; type in a letter or word in the Bookmark name box, then click the Add button. For some reason, you can't use words separated by spaces—which leads me to sometimes insert bookmarks such as "describebarn" or "describe-barn" so I'll know what it's about. In WordPerfect, you click Tools, then Bookmark, then Create, which lets you type in a name and say OK.

When you next open your document, to go to a bookmark you type control+g (PC) or apple+g (Mac), select Bookmark in the dialogue box that pops up, select the bookmark you want (there's a little arrow button to show a list of all bookmarks), click okay, and you're there.

Many uses

Let's say that you're really struggling with a passage, or maybe just chugging through the narrative, laying track, and you know what you've just written will need more thought. You can bookmark it and move on, knowing you can return with ease. Using bookmarks, I will revisit material that needs honing a number of times until I'm satisfied with it. With a bookmark, it's easy to go back and keep at it; without a bookmark, I suspect it would get far fewer visits and less thought.

Here's another one: deep into the umpteenth rewrite of a novel, it came to me that I needed to add a key visual and emotional element to a character's scenes in several places in the story. First, I inserted bookmarks at each scene where the new material was to be added (necklace1, necklace2, necklace3, etc.). Later, I jumped easily from one spot to another to make sure I had kept things consistent yet varied and had done all I needed to make the new material blend with the old. Because my first drafts tend to be on the lean side, bookmarking those additional bits of narrative enabled me to visit them after they'd cooled a little to see if they needed more work.

Because you can give each bookmark a different handle, another handy use is the ability to check back to important passages. This is especially useful for continuity checks. Let's say that early in the novel you created a detailed description of a room, and the things in that room are important to your story when they come up again. Put a bookmark there ("the-murder" or "crimescene" or some such) and it's easy to refer back and keep later references to that place accurate. This could be darned handy for clues in a mystery novel.

Bookmark the first page of each chapter to hop to one instantly. If you know you had Heather shoot the green bunny in chapter 4 but can't quite remember the sequence of events when you're referring to the shooting in chapter 16, it's easy to check.

Marking a passage for later use or change is another bookmark use. In one of my novels, I planned to move the description I'd written for a character to an earlier chapter during the rewrite. I bookmarked that passage so that when I got to the new description point in the rewrite, I could jump there, cut the description from its page, then jump back to where I was (because I inserted a "here" bookmark before I left that point) and paste it in. No hunting, no searching for keyword strings, etc.

nd so was the twin lawyers' aide,

Comment [RR1]: Should Patch's former associate be there and talk to him?

t to him. No Lester. And then there

Use the comment feature for better storytelling

Word's Comment feature is a hugely useful tool. You can insert an invisible note for yourself or someone else, such as an editor. When I was in an e-mail critique group, we used comments in our critiques along with line editing with Track Changes turned on. WordPerfect also offers a Comment tool.

I sometimes create a skeletal version of a scene that's not fully developed and use Comment to leave a note about thoughts for fleshing it out. Or maybe there's a description or action that I know needs work. In one of my novels I described a character as having a "pretty face." A critiquer rightly noted that this was vague—and it's an example of a "conclusion" word.

When I came to that place as I was rewriting, I just wasn't ready to deal with finding other language, so it was easy to highlight "pretty" and add this little note to myself: "better adjective/description—fine-boned, delicate features…" When I was good and ready, I took my time to do justice to the description.

> The woman's face emerged—oval shape, delicate features, and big eyes like you see in fashion models.

For me, that's one of the best uses for comments—to annotate possibilities that occur to me when I don't have the time or inclination to write them out. For example, in one scene the protagonist has left an intense but brief scene with his boss in which he quit his job. In the narrative I jumped ahead in time and simply wrote this:

> In his office, Gabe slammed the few personal things he didn't want to lose into his briefcase.

Then he left. Later, when skimming through the chapter, I had a nagging sense that the scene had ended too abruptly. So I highlighted "In his office" and added this comment: "consider having the boss following him into the hallway and finishing the confrontation." I went back later and created a much stronger scene. Here's the addition:

> Gabe was twenty feet down the hallway before Lawrence's voice attacked from behind. "You hold on there!"
>
> Gabe stopped and turned. Lawrence advanced on him, his face flushed, his hands clenched into fists.
>
> Lawrence came to a halt close enough for Gabe to smell the cigarette smoke in his breath. "What the fuck do you think you're doing?"
>
> Shackles lifted from Gabe's mind, and he felt strong and free. "How about the right thing?"
>
> Lawrence sucked in air as if Gabe had thrown a jab to his belly. His face reddened even more. "You're one more word from being out of a job."
>
> Out of a job. But this job, with Lawrence fouling his work and yanking on a leash, would be hell. Gabe had been there before, suffering the daily insult of working for a lesser man. Last time it had cost him lots of sleep and the beginnings of an ulcer. He'd vowed to never suffer fools again.
>
> One more word? Hell, he could do better than that. "Lawrence, don't you have ass-kissing to do? I think the client's going to need a long, deep pucker if you want to keep him happy."
>
> Like a fish, complete with glassy eyes, Lawrence opened and shut his mouth a couple of times. Then he spun and hurried back to the conference room. Gabe headed for his office, a flush of triumph thrumming through him.

There are different ways to add a comment. In Word 2000 and earlier, you highlight something where you want the comment to be, click Insert in the top menu, then click on Comment. A box will appear, you enter your note, then click Close. The comment becomes invisible until you want to see it, but yellow highlighting remains to show you where it is. You can insert a comment without highlighting anything, but I wouldn't—later there's no way to see where the comment is.

In Word 2002/XP, you insert comments in the same way. A comment balloon appears into which you type your comment. Annoyingly, the balloon stays there. To make it go away, go to View and click on Markup. Unfortunately, these versions of Word leave no highlighting to tell you where the comment is—you have to click on View/Markup.

In Word 2007, click on the Review tab in the ribbon and click on "New Comment."

There are two ways in Word 2000 and earlier to later view a Comment note. My preference is to place my cursor over the yellow highlight, which causes the comment to appear in a pop-up box. Move the cursor away, it goes away. Right-click your mouse (click the right key if you have a 2-key mouse) and you get a menu that will let you edit or delete the comment. An alternative way to view a Comment is to click View on the top menu in Word. Then click Comments, and a box will appear with all the comments in them. You can scroll to get to the area you want to see. This is a handy way to review all of the reminders you've left in order to see what needs to be done.

In Word 2002/XP, click View and then Markup to see comments. To make them go away, return to View and click Markup. In Word 2007, go to the Review tab. The default may be to display all comments and changes. To turn them off, click the Show Markup link and deselect whatever you don't want shown.

In WordPerfect, to insert a comment, click on Insert in the top menu bar, move your cursor to Comment, and click on Insert in the pop-up menu. To close the window that opens you have to click the X in the upper right corner. You can also navigate back and forth between your document and your comments with Window on the main menu bar.

WordPerfect adds small "word balloons" to the left margin of your document to indicate the presence of a comment. Click on the word balloon to read the comment. Right-click on the comment to edit or delete it.

About the author and his workshops

As it turns out, storytelling is my life. As a boy, when I read the *Book of Knowledge* the short stories and novellas were always the most fascinating parts. When I teened, I moved on to science fiction and fantasy via magazines such as *Analog* and *If* and a galaxy of mass market paperback books. SF and fantasy have been a constant in my reading ever since, although thrillers are my mainstay these days.

I also consumed comic books by the bale, which led to a desire to be a cartoonist—not in the sense of a style of art, but as a creator of drawn stories. As an adult, I created a couple of comic strips in hopes of becoming a professional cartoonist. Came close with one, but it wasn't to be (yet— there's a graphic novel growing in my mind). Some of the cartoons in this book are mine.

As a copywriter and then creative director (read: "editor") in advertising for twenty or so years, most of my seventy produced commercials were thirty-second stories, with beginnings, middles, and ends. My adverstorytelling propelled me to the top tier of the Chicago advertising scene.

While in advertising, another form of storytelling called to me: screenwriting. I left Chicago advertising to tackle screenwriting in Los Angeles and studied the craft in books, at UCLA, and at the American Film Institute. A few speculative screenplays later, I signed with an agent. But, while I could craft screen stories in a professional way, I never came up with a story that anyone wanted to invest millions in producing.

241

However, a two-minute animated Cap'n Crunch commercial from my advertising days that was, you guessed it, a story, helped me land a scriptwriting job at Filmation, one of the top Hollywood animation studios at the time. I became a story editor, writing scripts and editing the work of others. I have twenty half-hour screenplay credits from that gig. During that time, I also scripted a video adaptation of *The Little Engine that Could* for Universal Pictures—it's on the shelves in video stores.

But I moved on from that place and that job, re-entered advertising, ran into ageism, and began reinventing myself as an editor. Starting as a subcontractor for an online editing service, I edited beginner novels, and I became a member of the Editorial Freelancers Association and the Northwest Independent Editors Guild. I launched an online editing service in 2001, and have had modest success—I depend on a day job as a writer, editor, and video producer for a university to pay the serious bills.

As a form of guerilla marketing to generate editing work, in 2004 I started *Flogging the Quill,* a blog about the art and craft of storytelling. *FtQ* has become a popular "litblog" on the Internet: consistently in the top ten blogs on the Publishers Marketplace site; more than one hundred blogs link to it; and thousands of writers stop by every week for my coaching, essays on craft and storytelling, and critiques of writing.

While editing jobs have come to me as a result of the blog, the most satisfying part has been helping other writers conquer writing difficulties—you should see the delight in the thank-you notes I receive. I've also used the litblog as a springboard to doing editing workshops focused on storytelling at writer's conferences. More on that later.

And then there's the novelist side of me

I've completed five novels over the last ten years, learning as I go. A couple of them were viable enough to land a literary agent.

In terms of focus, I guess "commercial fiction" is mine, although I haven't settled into a single genre. So far my work doesn't conform to the expectations of genre fiction. As best as I can label them, my stories are:

➢ A speculative thriller
➢ A murder mystery set in the Old West
➢ A 1950s coming-of-age story with a mystery sub-plot
➢ A literary fantasy, set in contemporary America, which could also be considered a speculative thriller
➢ A satirical, tongue-in-cheek riff on the vampire myth

I don't know where I'll venture next—with luck, it will be dealing with the publication of one of the novels I'm shopping. I also hope to make the time for my graphic novel.

My education as a writer includes:

➢ Bachelor of science and master's in psychology
➢ Years of on-the-job learning at top advertising agencies
➢ On-the-job learning as a story editor in film
➢ Courses in script analysis and screenwriting at the American Film Institute
➢ The absorption of a gazillion books on the craft of writing novels and screenplays

Websites:

➢ Blog: www.floggingthequill.com
➢ Editing services and publishing company: www.FtQPress.com

The most helpful writing books on my bookshelves:

➢ *Story*, Robert McKee
➢ *On Writing*, Stephen King
➢ *Stein on Writing*, Sol Stein
➢ *Writing the Breakout Novel*, Donald Maass
➢ *Self-Editing for Fiction Writers*, Renni Browne and Dave King

Workshops

The workshops I do will evolve and change, but here are current options and interests.

Killer First Chapter, an online "tutorial" workshop. Four writers at a time work on their first twenty pages, with rewrites focusing on elements covered in this book: storytelling, description, dialogue, and technique. Workshoppers critique each others' work, as do I.

Killer First Page A writer's conference workshop based on my sixteen-line challenge for openings of novels—can you compel me to turn the page? Attendees submit their first chapter in advance, and then I lead the workshop in critiquing their first pages for "compellability" and craft.

Creating the Story Experience A conference workshop that includes writing exercises focused on writing for effect, experiential description, and dialogue action beats to create a narrative that evokes the story experience.

Editing

I offer what I call "story editing," an editing approach also called "line" editing and "substantive" editing. I'm not a copyeditor, although I will catch the huge majority of grammatical and punctuation shortcomings. My strengths are in story and narrative craft.

My editorial philosophy

I respect the writer's voice. I'll offer suggestions on wording, usually for reasons of clarity, meaning, or pace, but I do not rewrite to fit my way of saying things.

I aim to help writers achieve their intent—creating a story experience.

- ➤ If it's to describe, then to create description that evokes the scene.
- ➤ If to increase tension, then to help create crisp writing for effect that does the job well.
- ➤ If to characterize, then to help create nuances through action, description, and dialogue that bring a character to life.
- ➤ If to create a riveting plot, then to suggest twists, point out detours and going astray, to restructure—I've even suggested new endings for authors (which they used).

The things I work with writers on include

- ➤ Tightening the writing
- ➤ Story flow & pace, rooting out dead spots
- ➤ Plot flaws
- ➤ Continuity
- ➤ Staging action
- ➤ Description (that also characterizes)
- ➤ Character development
- ➤ Dialogue that moves the story
- ➤ Dialogue tags and action beats
- ➤ Transitions
- ➤ Use of active voice
- ➤ Proper word usage
- ➤ Clarity and weak word choices
- ➤ Overuse of words or characters
- ➤ Redundancies
- ➤ Spelling
- ➤ Sentence structure
- ➤ Coaching & instruction on writing craft

Free help for you

Unless demand exceeds supply of time and motivation, here are a couple of offers for writers who have bought this book and can provide proof of purchase as described below.

Free phone conference

I'll chat with you, or you and your critique group, about topics in the book or anything that's on your mind concerning writing. A half-hour for individuals, one hour for a group. You set up the call, and then we talk.

Free critique of your first 3 pages

If you bought this book, I'll give you a critique of the first three pages of your novel. It won't be an in-depth analysis like I would do for an edit, but you'll get some fresh eyes.

Here's how:

➢ "Proof" of purchase: Email to me a photo of you (and others, if you wish, such as your critique group) holding this book. Include in your email permission to use the picture on my website, and include your location. I'll keep names private if you wish.

➢ For a phone conference, email me for a day and time. Keep in mind that I'm in the Pacific time zone.

➢ For an evaluation, email the photo and a file attachment of the first three pages of your novel.

Index